"Read this book if you are looking for a gorgeous, theologically rich meditation on the incarnation. It will invite you to linger with the mystery of the God-Man by taking you through different scenes from Jesus's life and exploring how they shape our understanding of both divinity and humanity. This book is an invitation to fall more in love with Jesus."

—**Hannah Miller King**, Anglican priest; author of *Feasting on Hope*

"Kenneth Tanner is a true minister: someone who loves Jesus and loves people and writes from that love. Readers will feel that in *Vulnerable God*. I'm grateful for his consistent effort to both know the human Jesus better and help us know him too. Tanner invites us all, quite simply, to rest in our belovedness with a God who truly understands."

—**Meredith Miller**, pastor and bestselling author of *Wonder: 52 Conversations to Help Kids Fall in Love with Scripture*

"Kenneth Tanner looks squarely in the maw of mystery and survives both light and dark. A text of keen insight worthy of the read."

—**Thomas Lynch**, author of *The Undertaking*

"The Jesus you will meet in these pages is the human God, whose cruciform love is the face of God to a world in crisis. This Jesus is the living revelation that not one more person needs to die for the world to be put right."

—**Brad Jersak**, principal, St. Stephen's University; author of *A More Christlike God*

"In this beautiful, radical, original book, you will be taken closer and closer to the heart of God. And Tanner will take you there in the only way possible: in and through the vulnerable heart and healing wounds of Jesus Christ. If there was ever a contemporary

I0805651

book that understands and acts on Paul's insight that Christ crucified is, paradoxically, both the power of God and the wisdom of God, then this book is it. Accessible, mercifully free of jargon, and profoundly moving."

—**Malcolm Guite**, poet, priest, and life fellow of Girton College, Cambridge

"We've been handed a thousand images of a God made of cosmic power and heavenly distance. Kenneth Tanner offers us something far more terrifying, scandalous, and beautiful: a God who chose to be held. Tanner is doing what the best iconographers do—not explaining God but pointing the way until your eyes adjust and you finally see the vulnerable invitation to 'follow me.'"

—**Scott Erickson**, author of *Honest Advent* and *Say Yes*

"Too often we think that knowing God requires abstract formulas divorced from daily life. In earthy language, Kenneth Tanner describes a deeply hopeful possibility: that our ordinary human experience reveals not only our need for God but God himself, more like us than we dared hope. Read and find God as close as your own body."

—**Mandy Smith**, pastor and author of *Confessions of an Amateur Saint*

"The most important invitation for anyone who longs to know God is to contemplate Christ—to behold him in the fullness of who he is. But what does that actually mean? Enter Kenneth Tanner. In this book, we are given a beautiful and compelling vision of the humanity of Jesus, and, in turn, we discover how his humanity reveals to us the very heart and divinity of God."

—**Rich Villodas**, lead pastor, New Life Fellowship; author of *The Narrow Path*

VULNERABLE GOD

VULNERABLE GOD

How Jesus Upends Our Assumptions About God—and Shows Us How to Be Human

KENNETH TANNER

BrazosPress
a division of Baker Publishing Group
Grand Rapids, Michigan

Published by Brazos Press
a division of Baker Publishing Group
Grand Rapids, Michigan
BrazosPress.com

Printed in the United States of America

Library of Congress Cataloging-in-Publication Data

Names: Tanner, Kenneth, 1965– author

Title: Vulnerable God : how Jesus upends our assumptions about God—and shows us how to be human / Kenneth Tanner.

Description: Grand Rapids, Michigan : Brazos Press, a division of Baker Publishing Group, [2026] | Includes bibliographical references.

Identifiers: LCCN 2026007717 | ISBN 9781540902771 paperback | ISBN 9781493443352 ebook

Subjects: LCSH: Incarnation | Jesus Christ—Person and offices

Classification: LCC BT220 .T33 2026

LC record available at https://lccn.loc.gov/2026007717

Cover design by Laura Powell
Interior design by William Overbeeke

Cover image © *Christ of the Eucharist* by Lyuba Yatskiv, Icon Art Gallery

Published in association with The Bindery Agency, www.TheBinderyAgency.com.

Baker Publishing Group publications use paper produced from sustainable forestry practices and postconsumer waste whenever possible.

26 27 28 29 30 31 32 7 6 5 4 3 2 1

For Lela

Jesus is the sweetest name she knows

CONTENTS

A HUMAN DEATH

A HUMAN FUTURE

FOREWORD

Brian Zahnd

Jesus is God. Nothing is more central to the Christian faith than this confession. Christianity orbits around the audacious claim that the Galilean Jew known to history as Jesus of Nazareth was and is uniquely and fully divine. We insist that no matter how incongruent it may seem, the carpenter of Nazareth is also the Creator of the cosmos. In the most important of the ancient Christian creeds, we confess that Jesus Christ is "God from God, Light from Light, true God from true God."[1] But I suspect that most Christians misunderstand why this is so important.

In confessing the divinity of Christ, we do not mean that we already know what God is like—omnipotent, omniscient, omnipresent, omnibenevolent, all the theistic omnis put together—and that Jesus is *that*. No. We do *not* know what God is like. We don't begin with an abstract philosophical concept of God and then project it onto Jesus. Instead, we begin with Christ himself as the only way to know what God is truly like. In seeking to understand the transcendent Creator who dwells in unapproachable light, we cannot begin with "God" in abstraction as we will mostly end up with a divinized projection of our own aspirations, fears, values, and concepts of violent power. Which is to say, we have fashioned an idol.

At the end of the poetic prologue to his Gospel, John the Evangelist makes this daring assertion: "No one has ever seen God. It is the only Son, himself God, who is close to the Father's heart, who has made him known" (John 1:18). Think about what John has said. No one has ever seen God? We might protest. Didn't Abraham see God under the oaks of Mamre? Didn't Jacob see God at Bethel as the angels trafficked the ladder between heaven and earth? Didn't Moses see God on Mount Sinai so that his face shone? Aren't we told that Moses took the seventy elders of Israel up the mountain that they too might see God? Didn't Isaiah see God in the temple in the year King Uzziah died? Didn't Ezekiel have visions of God by the River Chebar? Yes, the Bible tells all these stories and more. And yet John is adamant—"No one has ever seen God." Why? Because no matter what dreams, visions, revelations, epiphanies, theophanies, or Christophanies people have had in times past, *compared to the revelation of God in Christ, no one has ever seen God!* Thus, the reason Christians confess the full deity of Christ is so that at last we might know what God is like. God is like Jesus! Or in the language of the New Testament, Jesus is "the exact imprint of God's very being" (Heb. 1:3). To see Jesus is once and for all to behold God and finally know what God is like. At the Last Supper, Jesus told his disciples who were requesting to see the Father, "Whoever has seen me has seen the Father" (John 14:9).

I know of nothing more central to Christian theology and Christian spiritual formation than a sustained meditation on Jesus Christ as the Word of God. The incarnation is the boundless mystery that should eternally fascinate our theological imagination. All Christian theology begins with wonder—and the greatest wonder of all is the eternal Logos assuming human flesh. Why does the Word of God enter the world through a human birth? "In order that the world might be saved through him" (John 3:17). The world will not be saved by political movements or various activisms. This is the folly of the culture wars—or of all wars, for that matter. The crucified and risen Word of God may, at times, inspire movements and activism, but we must not imagine that Christ is a mere accessory to our political or social agendas. Christ is not an addendum; Christ is the Alpha and the Omega. All things have been created by and for Christ. He is the origin and telos of all creation. In pronouncing that all things are created by and for Christ, and that all things in heaven and on earth are reconciled in Christ, the apostle Paul begins his lofty christological hymn by first telling us that Jesus "is the image [icon] of the invisible God" (Col. 1:15). Jesus is the perfect icon of the invisible God. We are no longer guessing in abstraction concerning what God is like—we now gaze upon the icon who is Christ and move toward the beatific vision.

I know Kenneth Tanner, and I know he loves icons. You will find icons in his domestic and ecclesial habitats. He speaks frequently of icons and has given small replicas of the famous Sinai Pantocrator to many a soul. I am a grateful recipient of one of these gifts. And Kenneth Tanner is an iconographer himself. No, he doesn't work with egg tempera and gold leaf on wooden panels, but he is an iconographer, nonetheless. Tanner is a pastor-theologian who works with the medium of words. In *Vulnerable God*, we find a valuable and beautiful sustained meditation on Jesus Christ. This book does not read like a dry, academic, theological tome—it is far more like a poetic portrait. Thankfully, this book does not join the ranks of the ubiquitous catalogs of Christian pragmatism in which we are told "how to" do this or that. This book simply invites us to gaze upon the face of Christ until the miracle of inner transformation begins to occur. Christ does the saving; all we have to do is look upon him. "Turn to me and be saved" (Isa. 45:22). This book is not angry—we have far too many of those. This book is gracious. It doesn't strike as lightning; it falls as a gentle rain. *Vulnerable God* as a sustained meditation on the implications of the incarnation draws regularly upon ancient Christian theologians and pastors, but Tanner does it in such a way that Origen, Athanasius, and others feel bracingly contemporary.

What I love most about this book is that every single page is about Jesus. Yes, *every single page!* This is why I describe *Vulnerable God* as an icon, and Kenneth Tanner as a theological iconographer. Page after page we are invited to look upon Christ—as a helpless infant, as a curious adolescent, as a young carpenter, as an itinerant healer, as a humble servant, as one crucified and buried, as one risen and ascended. Through this literary icon, we are invited to look upon the vulnerable God who sustains the cosmos with his word and fills all things everywhere with himself. Read this icon and behold the beauty of the Lord.

A HUMAN GOD

No one can look at God and at the reality of the world with undivided gaze as long as God and the world are torn apart. Despite all efforts to prevent it, the eyes still wander from one to the other. Only because there is one place where God and the reality of the world are reconciled with each other, at which God and humanity have become one, is it possible there and there alone to fix one's eyes on God and the world together at the same time. This place does not lie somewhere beyond reality in the realm of ideas. It lies in the midst of history as a divine miracle. It lies in Jesus Christ the reconciler of the world.

—Dietrich Bonhoeffer, *Ethics*

The growing good of the world is partly dependent on unhistoric acts; and that things are not so ill with you and me as they might have been, is half owing to the number who lived faithfully a hidden life.

—George Eliot, *Middlemarch*

Only the devil
disguising himself
as Christ
has no wounds, being too vain to bear them.

—a saying of the desert fathers

MYSTERY

I am lying on an emergency room gurney surrounded by a resuscitation team. My heart rate is spiking well over two hundred beats per minute.

A young doctor whom I recognize walks in and says, "I'm going to inject you with something that's going to stop your heart . . . but only for a moment. It's going to feel weird for a second or two, but I promise it will start back up."

I had met this young doctor weeks before. Outside the parish I serve in San Clemente, a newly engaged couple had been out for dinner. It wasn't clear what happened after. A gang approached their car, words were exchanged, the man unwisely exited the vehicle, and in the confrontation that ensued, he was stabbed.

I walk up to the scene of his blood splattered fiancée, a lit-up ambulance, and a gathering of first responders.

A priest's collar makes one visible in ways plain clothes do not, and the woman gravitates to me, pleading and clinging. A paramedic asks if I can accompany her to the hospital.

There is a concerted effort to save the man, but the knife has punctured his heart. They put me in another room with the woman.

"Why him? Why us? We are in love. We were having a beautiful evening. He's a beautiful man. Why, Father?"

The young trauma doctor emerges from behind the curtain, weary and dejected, and delivers the news no one ever wants to hear. "We're sorry. We did all we could. The wound wasn't survivable." She clings to me and wails . . . for a long time.

I know that wail.

I heard it the first time before I turned five. Some soldiers showed up at our front door and took away a vital joy at the heart of my mother that she never got back. My sisters and I were fatherless.

You can try to submerge that wail of loss. You want it to stop, not only because a woman in anguish is not the way the world is supposed to be but also because you want this particular woman in front of you, the one clinging to you, to have her joy back.

The young trauma doctor is right: My heart starts back up after the injection, but my pulse remains rapid and irregular. It takes about a day to get my heart calm and back in sinus rhythm.

Weeks later, I am sitting in the office of a Croatian internist, a Catholic, with a receding hairline and abundant gray eyebrows, who slowly rubs his hands together in silence. He is running his left hand through his right hand and then his right hand through his left hand as if washing them. He sits opposite me. He says nothing.

He is at least thirty years older than me. White jacket. A stethoscope around his neck. He looks at me with intention, his eyes on mine, silent.

After a minute or so, he stops rubbing his hands together and says, "Why are you so anxious? You work for God."

I have no answer for his question. *Why am I so anxious?*

I *have* seen a lot of death. That winter, on a Sunday morning about dawn, on my way to a parish I serve in the high desert, I came on the scene of a motorcycle accident on one of Ortega Highway's sharp turns. A young man lay in the roadway. Still helmeted, he had snapped his neck on impact. At his friends' request, I said prayers over his body, holding his gloved hand.

My doctor breaks his silence again. He asks me, "Do you pray the psalms?" I begin to wonder what sort of physician this is but reply, "No, not really." I do, of course, in daily and weekly services at the church where I serve as a priest. But I take him to mean do I *personally*. He says, "You should. They will help you to encounter the face of Jesus."

He prescribes some heart medications, talks about exercise and diet, but his main advice is "contemplate Christ."

Ponder Christ in all things. I take this advice. I begin to contemplate the person of Jesus Christ. That contemplation has only just begun, but it has changed my life. Pondering the person of Christ centers me in the present moment and gives me hope. This book is about my experiences of Jesus Christ—what I have seen, heard, read, and felt—on the way that never ends: the journey to becoming human as God is human.

We are tempted to think of Jesus along the lines of a metahuman, impervious to most of what harms us, virtually indestructible. Yet Jesus is nothing like that.

When God is revealed as human, a quiet, wondrous mystery takes shape in the womb of a Judaean teenager: Jesus takes on our shatterable, earthenware humanity. Jesus is vulnerable to all our frailties. He can be crushed by stoning, burned by fire, weakened by lack of water, food, or sleep. He is susceptible to cuts, bruises, bacteria, radiation, and gravity.

His cause of death is likely exsanguination, bleeding out in agony and disgrace, without resistance or appeal to a violent defense.

Out of this weakness, Jesus is somehow strong in ways we struggle to grasp. This is a power we do not know (though we are created to desire it).

As it turns out, Jesus is both more human and more divine than I imagined. Indeed, my understanding of "human" and "divine" are altered by my encounters with Christ. My perceptions are, even as I write this, too small-minded and too small-hearted.

I am small and Christ is great. My mind and heart cannot contain the treasures of this One who holds all things together, who is reconciling all things to himself. Jesus is the mystery at the heart of existence.

Jesus is the mystery at the heart of existence.

In Christian tradition, a mystery is not a puzzle to solve but something we get glimpses of, get impressions of, see visions of—something so great we are not able to hold or contain it. We sputter to put words to it. We must at some point leave the vastness of it alone in our attempts to say something about it. This book is but an attempt.

There are many beautiful mysteries in the story of Jesus. We can and will say some things about them, and the gathering of Christ followers through time has agreed on some things that we all say together about the story of the human God who belongs to all humans. I am particularly drawn to the witness of the first Christians. Yet every time we gaze on Jesus Christ, we see more than all that has been said.

It's vital to pay attention to what moves us, what bring tears of joy to the eyes and, amid conflicts of every kind, an inexplicable peace to the soul. These moments are witnesses. They are interruptions, a *kērygma* (cry of announcement) within us that the God who is always nearer to us than we are to ourselves is no figment, no projection, but right here, appearing among us now and everywhere present.

One such story for me involves the Estonian composer Arvo Pärt. In a time of occupation, under a shroud of imposed atheism, Pärt remembers trying to compose music in a "monastery's yard, on a bench, in the shadow of the bushes."[1]

A little girl approaches him and asks him what he is writing in his notebook. "I'm trying to write music," he tells her, "but it's not turning out well."

The little girl replies, "Have you thanked God for this failure already?"

Every time I hear Pärt recount this story I weep, and something somewhere inside me touches the permanent. I remember that my capacities and efforts as a pastor and theologian are limited—my wisdom is meager, my sight dim, my ear dull. Then I remember that humility is what holds everything in breath and in motion, and I thank God for my failure.

We too often discount experience in telling the story of the human God, forgetting that those who followed Jesus had living contact with him—his touch on their skin, his voice in their ears—before speaking of him. They felt his love before they wrote of it. What we have experienced of Jesus is vital to telling our story and his.

When theology is divorced from our lived connection with a living God, when it is abstracted from the real world of blood, iron, wood, fire, water, earth, and air, it can be boring, irrelevant, confusing, uninspiring, and (sometimes) deadly.

This book is about seeking the face of God in the real world of pain. It's about soldiers who show up at the front door and tell us our father is dead, about what happened to my mother in that moment, about how disintegrating those words were to her, about my trying to hold her, to somehow get her back together, wanting the nightmare to end, wanting her not to suffer in that way for another moment.

The soldiers' news brought my father's mother, to whom this book is dedicated, into the center of my childhood. I spent a lot of weekends with her and my grandfather. He was a disabled carpenter, and she worked in a factory.

They and the folks who filled their church were everyday, earthy saints. We sang nineteenth-century hymns about Christ's blood and wounds, and spoke in tongues, and loved Jesus. Experiencing Jesus was at the center of their day-to-day lives. Reading the Scriptures, being with the poor, singing into the night—so much singing—lots of exuberance, lots of joy, lots of tears, all of it was about intimate connection with Jesus. That's the soil in which my faith in Jesus grew.

My mother and stepfather took us into charismatic renewal in my late adolescence and teens, in its beginnings part of a beautiful, vital reunion that occurred around the Holy Spirit with Christians from all sorts of churches.

I ended up at Oral Roberts University, with love for the Pentecostal formation of my grandparents but with growing suspicion of the idea that a Christian is someone who "makes it" in life, who escapes being poor or being sick. That if you are suffering, according to some teachers, you are somehow disobedient to God or your faith is weak.

Then midway through my second year, the space shuttle *Challenger* explodes during liftoff and the entire campus walks into chapel just moments later. The pastoral leader of the community gets up, mentions the disaster, but says we are going to leave "that" outside the walls of Kennedy Chapel because we are here to praise Jesus. I enjoy singing, but loud exuberance seems out of touch with the collective loss we are experiencing. I sit down in silence, not able to articulate my discomfort.

Fifteen minutes later, a preacher takes the pulpit, a theologian named Charles Farah, who begins by telling us that his wife of decades died of cancer the year before. He says that as he and Jo Ann navigated the trial of her illness, they began to experience, each in their own way, Christ suffering with them and—this arrested me—they each came to feel they were somehow participating in the sufferings of God on the cross.

Here was a trust I could hold on to: a God who agonizes alongside all who suffer, not only by his own human trials and temptations in the flesh but also by entering all our hardships with us whenever we are afflicted. While we seek to escape our body of suffering, our Creator is acquainted with embodied grief.

A few weeks after Farah's sermon, I read in Irenaeus, one of the first Christian pastors, how God becomes human to join us in the human predicament; that God desires not to destroy the world—for the earth is not evil!—but to reclaim the good creation that he made good. Irenaeus says that God becomes human to rescue not only my soul but also my body—indeed, the souls and bodies of all humans—from death (*Against Heresies* 5.1.3; 5.3.2–3; 5.21.1; 5.36.1).

The escapism of my childhood churches, accompanied by constant scares about a rapture and the ever-looming end of the world, never seemed authentic. As I listened to the first Christians, I heard them tell a different story about God and the world that made sense and felt right.

I discovered (and continue to discover) that Christianity has many traditions other than the one in which I was raised, that the waters of Christian reflection and practice are deeper and their wisdom more radiant than can be explored or beheld in a lifetime.

In the words of the first Christians about the human God, in bread and wine on a table, in transfiguring icons and radiant hymns, and in the poor, prisoners, and immigrants I met—in all these and in so much more—I was encountering Jesus.

As I learned (and continue to learn) to read Scripture with this wonderful mosaic of humans and joined the time-tried prayers of many eras, tribes, tongues, and places, humility about my tiny grasp of the immensities settled somewhere in me somehow over time, and on my better days, humility keeps me in awe and joy.

The first Christians held a weekend remembrance of the death and resurrection of Jesus that eventually grew to a yearlong cycle of feasts and fasts called the sacred year. Much of the language of this book (indeed, its very structure) comes from the experience of celebrating this sacred year around a table of bread and wine in a gathered community devoted to prayer, teaching, and fellowship with the poor.

Practicing this sacred year helps us see that all moments of the human God in time are available to every moment of time—past, present, and future—and that all the events of Christ's life among us are always at work for us and in us.

As we enter the sacred year in the chapters that follow, we will inhabit moments from Jesus's story and ask: What does this human life among us show us about God? How does this divine life among us reshape our way of being human?

Churches that observe the sacred year are often called "liturgical." They practice the liturgy, which imitates the ancient pattern of synagogue worship and is wedded to a compression of the Passover meal called the Eucharist. I will refer to liturgical practices throughout this book, but if you are not from a liturgical tradition, this book is still for you. Indeed, all these practices—including the sacred year—belong to all humans.

Throughout this book, I hope to introduce you to some of the ancient and contemporary voices that help me contemplate Jesus. If you tend to skip quotations, I encourage you to read them. You will get more from this book if you take those extra moments.

I use a theological shorthand throughout this book, referring to Jesus as "the human God." I often simply use the word "God" to name Jesus Christ. It's a deliberate choice to counter a stubborn refusal to profess Jesus Christ, our human brother, as the One we mean to always and everywhere invoke whenever we use the word "God."

This shorthand is never meant to circumscribe. It is meant to affirm a vital mystery: There is only one God, the Father, the Almighty, and one Lord Jesus Christ, the only Son of God—God from God, Light from Light—the Word who is with God and who is God, who with the Spirit is sent into the world by the Father.

This is the simplest way I have found to say what a contemplative encounter with Jesus has taught me: God makes the world in love. God loves the world God makes. God becomes what God makes to die for the world God loves. And the end of all things is the world at last healed and made one with the Love John calls God, the forever human Jesus of Nazareth.

It is vital to tell the story of the human God as well as we can because it is the story of Jesus that makes sense of God and humanity.

Contemplation of the human God is good for you and for the world. It does not need to lead to anything "practical." Loitering with the person of Jesus Christ is beneficial all by itself. Loiter awhile with me.

BASIN

Our closest galactic neighbor, Andromeda, is 2.5 million light-years away. She dwarfs our galaxy and contains a trillion stars. The energy that fuels all those stars and has kept them in a vast spiral for ten billion years is measurable, but who has the instruments or the time? The best we can do is make estimates.

Our witness and wisdom say that a first-century baby born to a peasant Jewish teenager, a baby whose stepfather was a carpenter, is the One who spoke the originating components of this galaxy into fiery substance and perpetual motion way back when. And our tradition claims that this human is the One who spoke another hundred billion galaxies into existence from nothing that existed before . . . *ex nihilo* in the ancient tongue.

We read in Scripture that on the night before he suffered on a cross for the cosmos he created, Jesus took a towel and a basin of water and washed the grimy feet of his friends. You do not wash someone's feet without getting low to the ground, without kneeling before them, without bowing your head to them, without risking intimacy with them, without becoming vulnerable to them. In the world of Christ's time, the host of a meal would never be the one to wash the feet of his guests.

When Jesus wraps a towel around his waist and washes the feet of his disciples, the Son of God gives us a portrait of someone unseen, whom he calls Father, the One who with Christ and the Spirit holds all things together—visible and invisible—an image of God as unassuming, humble servant.

When we dare to mess around with the deep structures by which God holds the visible universe together—splitting atoms, for instance—we witness the dreadful energy generated by our manipulations of God's handiwork. Christ reveals that this incalculable power—even the smallest fraction of it leaves us in awe when we catch a glimpse of its potential—is harnessed to an extreme humility.

Divine humility, revealed in the flesh of Jesus Christ, is the uncreated source of all the creative energy in the cosmos.

This divine humility, revealed in the flesh of Jesus Christ, is the uncreated source of all the creative energy in the cosmos. This washing of feet shows that the power of God has its purpose not in what fallen human imagination supposes—not in great demonstrations of subatomic or interstellar force—but in innumerable divine acts of indiscriminate, behind-the-scenes, and expensive love.

Our human God cares for all things, great and small, from what may even seem useless to us—the things we would throw away—to things of such exquisite beauty we are left without words.

God is the One among us who serves, kneeling on the floor of the universe, towel in hand, ready to do the menial work that binds all things together, the work of a love that does not seek attention, does not boast, is not rude or jealous, keeps no record of wrongs, does not fail.

What does it mean that the One who creates all stars and fuels their fires is on his knees, serving humans in vulnerable intimacy? Let me suggest that most human projection of what it means to be a god or "God"—and most human imagination of what it means to be truly powerful—has been deeply and damagingly mistaken.

The sorts of gods we project, whether in ancient lore or in our contemporary cinematic universes, are usually the sorts that wield "powers" to control persons or outcomes. They might change the nature of things or trespass boundaries to suit their ends, but they are not the living God revealed in the Scriptures.

Jesus reveals God as poor. He is the child of a worker-woman, born into a carpenter's household, birthed in a cave or shelter with other earthen creatures and their shite—not in a place where the wealthy dwell—not only as a judgment on the ways in which we exalt ourselves into superior ranks, separating ourselves from others by positions and attainments, but also because he means to reveal to us the binding truth of God's sacred inferiority.

If in Christ God had come among us as a human of status or influence or strength, we would have a misunderstanding of who God is in eternity. We would forget that God is small.

Celsus, an ancient Roman critic of Jesus and his gospel, helps us remember something the first Christians took for granted: "Since a divine Spirit inhabited the body [of Jesus], his body must certainly have been different from that of other beings, in respect of grandeur, or beauty, or strength, or voice, or impressiveness, or persuasiveness, . . . whereas Jesus was, as [the Christians] report, little, and ill-favored, and insignificant."[1] Seeking to foil anyone who might be attracted to the Christian faith, Celsus argues that the story of the first Christians is foolish. After all, smart and sophisticated humans look for signs of divinity in physical beauty, charisma, and stature.

If the invisible Spirit who gives all things life and movement were to join himself to human flesh, then surely, Celsus says, that person would look like our usual projections of divine and human strength . . . someone like Adonis or Zeus.

We are not so different from the ancients. Look at the gods we have assembled in, for example, the Marvel Cinematic Universe. They are handsome, fit, strong, resourceful practitioners of disciplined, old-school aggression. If they're not endowed with cosmic powers or the capacity to harness nature in some unique way, they're superintelligent with sophisticated technological exoskeletons or are trained experts in mystical or martial arts.

Superheroes are easy on the eye, clever, muscular—and violent, capable of imposing their will. The gospel tells us that the weakness of Jesus Christ—the vulnerability of humanity and divinity that meet in his unique person—is infinitely stronger than our notions of power. We can't see that by looking at him, however.

Humanity's actual God is not an alien humanoid like Superman, impervious to harm, but someone like all of us who bleeds and sweats, who endures ridicule, torture, and agonizing death. Short of stature or not, Jesus was not striking. He did not stand out. In Jesus Christ, God takes upon God all of the myriad ways in which all of us are disabled. He was despised and, as Isaiah tells us, disfigured beyond recognition in his death (Isa. 52:14; 53:3).

Being the Suffering Servant is not a temporary way of life for God; it is subversively permanent. We struggle to imagine this is who God is among us and in eternity, but Jesus is the overthrow of everything we think we know about God and humanity.

Our desire to be powerful leads to self-deception and is the surest way to forget that God is the gardener we executed, the shepherd we forsook, the physician we rejected, who yet loves us and the world. If we were as small as God, we would understand these things. Jesus wants to help us by showing us the way to be small as God is small.

This story of a God who washes feet tells us that if we want to encounter God in this world, we might consider spending time with janitors and waitresses, with nurses and firemen, with doormen and midwives. The way of the cross, the path of humility and co-suffering love, leads to life *through* death, where every impediment to joining Love's care for all things is burned from us like straw in flame. On this narrow path, we become ever-descending servants of the cosmos—we become like God, the selfless steward. Our defenseless power is bent knees and wash basins.

Some speak of the cross in ways we can and should forget, a cross that is a brief stop of surrender and selflessness on a violent crusade toward a "greatness" that makes Jesus a kind of forever Caesar. In this scenario, Christ's "humility" leads to an eternal tyranny, to world domination without end.

Jesus dies precisely as God in God's fullness, as the first of us to become fully and finally human, not as a tyrant but as an afflicted servant-king, for only the wounded God can save and rule the world.

It takes the whole dangerous road to and through death to become human; surviving isn't part of the equation for this kind of love—resurrection is. Self-defense doesn't come into it, not even when the moment of truth comes. God's self-giving love will not be and need not be shielded from our violence. Bearing wounds in powerlessness is the very nature of this human God—the nature of any greatness.

A few years ago, a young man went kayaking on Lake Michigan. He told his girlfriend he wanted to spend some time in the open with God. Jacob Sandy had paddled out a distance when a supercell thunderstorm formed. As I sat across from his sister after his body was found, she recalled how on the day that Jacob died, she and her mother were gardening. It was sunny and beautiful in her backyard while her brother was alone in the middle of a dark storm.

After sitting for a time and listening to her lament, I shared with her my trust that Jacob was not alone. Jesus was with Jacob—not simply alongside him in the cold water or hovering somewhere above the calamity but somehow in Jacob, drowning with him.

Consider this, from Orthodox theologian Sergius Bulgakov: "We can say that in . . . the fullness of Christ's dying, the death of every human and of all humanity is included. If Christ redeems and raises every person, then it is only because he co-dies in every person and with every person. It therefore follows that Christ, glorified and sitting at the right hand of the Father, even now suffers and dies with the humanity whose collective suffering and death he once took upon himself and exhausted on Golgotha."[2]

And further still: Jesus descends into all our hells. The descent of Jesus is not slowed until he is beneath the deepest falling human, descending right to the edges of nonexistence to rescue us. Any human who hits rock bottom lands on the body of Christ. There is no other place to land.

One of the pastors of the first Christians, Athanasius, says in *Contra Gentes* (41.2) that God is not stingy with existence. Jesus wants his fellow humans to participate in his never-ending divine life. He gives humans not the virtual permanence of Andromeda but his own permanence, and with us somehow also grants the cosmos this great gift of his eternity.

As a fellow human, Jesus is our mediator and advocate. He is made like his brothers and sisters in every way so that he might be the One who rules and judges those whose existence he understands from the inside; he lived our human story with us in the most vulnerable, authentic, and beautiful way.

What the God who is human has done no other god has done nor can do: He has entered into all of our deprivations and taken upon himself all the evils we endure in order not only to triumph over them but to bear them as we do.

He does not stand outside our lacks and sufferings but humbly experiences them with us by his sufferings as a contingent death-bearing human. And he bears our share of sorrow, too, so that we never suffer without him right there inside it with us.

In Jesus, God has a mother and a betrayer. In Jesus, God has scars and memories—of meals and laughter with his friends and nights huddled together against the desert air in cloaks, of storms at sea and a grinding emptiness at the tomb of his friend.

In Jesus, God knows hunger and thirst and loneliness and pain. In Jesus, God knows the human devastation of divorce and disease and death. In Jesus, the One who's been given all authority in heaven and on earth is one of us.

It is the weakness of God in the human flesh of Jesus that saves the cosmos God loves. Let this mind be in you that is also in Christ Jesus, who took upon his eternity our every disability, who lived among us as a servant, who went silent to his execution, so that the world might live.

Jesus is the name above all names because the One who serves all things in creation is at once the revelation of what it means to be human and of what it means to be God.

God has DNA. God grows tired and thirsty. God has an executioner. God bleeds and God dies. These are sentences of Christian trust because the one person Jesus Christ is not God in some ways and human in other ways but at once divine and human in all things.

In Jesus Christ, to stop being human is to stop being God, and to stop being God is to stop being human, because in Jesus Christ there is no distance or disharmony between remaining human and remaining God. In him, they are forever one and the same thing.

The Son of God is human from eternity, but the story we tell about him begins in a small village. Here, a young woman consents to bear humanity's vulnerable God, and the giver of indestructible life becomes breakable. It is to that baffling, magnificent beginning that we now turn.

FLESH

All things—seen and unseen, earthly and heavenly, physical and metaphysical, goodness, truth, and beauty as well as stars and seas, the birds of the air and the beasts of the field—were *breathed* into existence by the Word who is with God and is God.

Here is a great mystery: Crucified human and divine weakness made the universe from nothing by speaking it into existence (Gen. 1:3–25). As Athanasius teaches, it is the crucified, wounded Savior who creates all things, even though that messes with our notions of sequence, time, and the eternal (*Contra Gentes* 2.2).

By contrast, God *formed* human beings from the dust, handcrafting humanity from clay, breathing into us, male and female, "the breath of life" (Gen. 2:7).

Our God-modeled flesh, invested with his image, was made alive by the Spirit with a spark of God's own liveliness. We were given the gift of language so that we might enter the divine conversation.

All things exist in this give-and-take communion. All things communicate. Only humans, however—uniquely formed to meet with God face-to-face, breathing the very breath of the

Word—have the gift of words. If we are like God, our words are creative; if we are not, our words destroy. "Death and life," the Scriptures say, "are in the power of the tongue" (Prov. 18:21).

The mystery of the incarnation is so great that every year during Advent and Christmas, Lent and Easter, we see something we have never seen before, encountering by the Spirit a facet of the narrative that we missed or neglected or left unsung.

So, as if for the first time, ponder the humility of a God who speaks all things into existence from nothing making himself speechless, making himself incapable of sounding words, by coming to us as a womb-bound and wordless creature.

Ponder the playfulness and audacity of a God who invites a teenager to share in the inner workings of sovereignty.

Ponder the fact that in her womb, thanks to her yes and amen, the Son who sang the far-flung galaxies into motion eons ago comes to complete silence, the uncontainable Word wordlessly knit together in that earthen space, a space hardly larger than a pear or apple.

Ponder that this Word emerges from her womb into this world of struggle and pain and vulnerability in utter dependence. Beyond crying out, as most babies do, and apart from the glory of his simply being there in need, the eternally begotten Son, now cradled to Mary's breast, has no power to address his human brothers and sisters.

Words like *immah* (mother) and *abba* (father), Jesus learns from Mary. The One who would later say, "I am the door," "I am the bread of life," "I am the light of the world," "I am the resurrection and the life" first cooed and bawled like any healthy baby does. For years and years, his words, to say nothing of his bearing, gave no indication of his majesty—the mystery of divinity and humanity that is spoken in Jesus Christ.

So much—infinity, no less—can be spoken without words in the flesh of this speechless Son. Yet this great mystery, the mystery of God, the mystery of existence itself, *is* worded, surrounded by conversation, song—and music.

The Word who spoke all things into being lets his creatures speak when he cannot, and say of him what he must learn to be true about himself—by listening to the voice of the teenager who welcomed him to be born in her.

Here is a creaturely word spoken of the uncreated Word: The wingèd archangel Gabriel brings a mystifying message to Mary, an invitation from thrice-holy Love, a request to bear in her the divine Word by whom in the beginning the Father spoke the cosmos into existence by the Spirit.

And Mary consents: "Here am I, the servant of the Lord; let it be with me according to your word" (Luke 1:38). Mary does not forget Love but remembers in faith that she is made by Love from dust.

The Spirit hovers over her as over the waters in Genesis, and a new creation is conceived in Mary's womb by the conversation that unfurls, but not by their conversation alone. The words of the prophets, the words of the psalmists, the words of the saints—these too are drawn by the Spirit into making all things new within and by her. We confess with Lucy Peppiatt that "Jesus is made of [Mary], not just in her. He is made from her and not just through her. Mary is not simply a receptacle of the divine, housing him, as it were. She supplies his humanity from her own body."[1]

The mystery of the gospel is a *worded* mystery. The Word is made flesh, and the words of Scripture give flesh to the Word. In the Word made flesh, all the words of Scripture find the tongue that interprets them.

The glorious mystery is sung as well as spoken, not only by the angels to the shepherds but also by Mary, who teaches her child to sing psalms like this one: "I waited patiently for the Lord; he inclined to me and heard my cry. He drew me up from the desolate pit, out of the miry bog, and set my feet upon a rock, making my steps secure. He put a new song in my mouth, a song of praise to our God. Many will see and fear and put their trust in the Lord" (Ps. 40:1–3).

In the Word made flesh, all the words of Scripture find the tongue that interprets them.

We are told this psalm was written by David, the ancestor of Mary and Jesus, a shepherd and poet in Israel, a warrior, Israel's true king. His praise, like all true praise, was born of his experience of God.

His people heard in his praise the sound of their hope, so they took it to heart. Generation after generation they sang it, until they couldn't *not* sing it. Mary and Joseph learned this song and then taught it to Jesus long before they knew in the fullest sense that he, their son, was truly David's Lord.

Jesus grew up with this song. He sang it and kept singing it, and in time it became clear to him the song was about him, that all the songs were. At some point, he came to know that he himself was the song his people sang.

Jesus knew himself as we are all meant to know ourselves. He recognized the truth of himself in ways we for now cannot. What we do know is that Jesus is the truth of ourselves. We know that Jesus is the song we are all meant to sing. We know this because every line of Scripture becomes music when we hear the words in the voice of Jesus Christ. Listening to that music, we are moved to the same praise that moved David to sing.

Whatever passage of Scripture we are reading and meditating on, we must ask how it not only speaks *of* Jesus but also is him speaking *to* us. We are invited to ask: How is the One who is baptized in the Jordan and tempted in the wilderness, sleeps in a boat and is laid to rest in a tomb, kneels in Gethsemane and is nailed to a tree—how is it that he is given flesh and blood by these words?

Then, without pretending to know the answer, we must sit in the silence until we hear the song of Christ rising in our hearts.

At just the right moment in the human story, when God unveiled God within our tangible and contingent existence, God became human.

Some of us have been led to believe this becoming was unbecoming for God. In truth, however, nothing is more fitting for the Word than for him to be human. Indeed, it is quite simply who he is.

Assuming flesh, he becomes what he loves from all eternity. And he becomes not just a human being but humanity itself. He is, as only he can be, human *for all of us* and *in all of us*, the image of the likeness we bear, the light that enlightens everyone who comes into the world.

God does not become what he does not love. God does not become what he hates. God becomes what God has made good. This is a solidarity exceeded only by his willingness to die for those of us who have hated him.

"God saw everything that he had made, and indeed, it was very good" (Gen. 1:31). What God makes good can never lose its bedrock created-in-goodness virtue, however broken it becomes. God is not and cannot be a failed Creator.

Let me say it again: In becoming human, God becomes what is inherently good. God cannot become what is by nature evil. This is simple, but in our broken state we forget the simple things.

Despite what we have too often been told, humans do not have a "sin nature." We have a human nature afflicted by sin, an infection that is at war with our goodness, a disease that eats away at the divine-human image of God in us.

God forever is love, and humans are made in the image of that love, made to love as God loves. So love, not sin, is elemental to us humans. Sin is alien and hostile to us. A basic claim of the first Christians and their Judaic heritage is that human nature is not inherently evil but rather participates in an original created goodness now wounded by sin.

The image of God and the image of all humans is the human God, Jesus Christ, nailed to wood. Every human is, by virtue of being God's creation, good—fashioned "by hand" in the image of love, not hate; in the image of generosity, not greed; in the image of welcome, not exile; in the image of healing, not harm; in the image of humility, not pride.

While the sin of Adam has wide-reaching destructive consequences for everyone and everything, Christians trust that the obedient life of the human God is far, far greater than Adam's transgression. As Paul writes, "For as all die in Adam, so all will be made alive in Christ" (1 Cor. 15:22). Irenaeus echoes the apostle: "The Lord . . . [made himself] the beginning of those who live, as Adam became the beginning of those who die."[2] The sinlessness of Jesus Christ is greater than the collective sin of humanity. Christ's way of being human will override every evil in us and in creation. This is a basic Christian trust. And that trust can and must change the way we look at everyone and the way we see everything. Jesus is the lens through which we behold reality. He is our vision.

When God becomes human, he takes on human nature as he finds it, subject to the conditions of a broken world, for what has not been assumed has not been redeemed. But a bridgehead of goodness remains in every human, no matter how many layers of soot mar this incandescent reality.

Ancestral sin is real. We see its effects everywhere and in all. Sin is a power that afflicts us, no doubt about it. But it is important to recall that we are not our sins. They are not constitutive of our identity. They do not define us or determine our destiny. The human God does.

While we seek to escape human frailty, contingency, danger, hunger, thirst, suffering, and death, God becomes human and embraces all our poverties. The Word becomes a helpless, speechless, fragile baby born without privilege to a working family, a family forced to live under a cloud of suspicion and accusation because of the circumstances of his conception. He assumes the one nature all humans share, a nature subject for now to the desperations of this world, a nature bound to death.

God's purpose is to lend all of us—we who have fallen from the community of Love, we who are infected with death, we who have descended into hell and the grave—his eternity.

The only way that God could arrest and reverse our descent into non-being, into nothingness, was to become human, to live toward death as one of us, dying so that he, the God who chooses to be human, could fall with falling humanity, gripping our collective wrist as he rises again, to lift us all back into a blessedness that exceeds Eden.

Mary comes to know herself as chosen, as sacred, as ark, as prophet, as witness, as portal, as magnified—as *Theotokos*, God-bearer, Mother of God and the new Eve, the mother of all the living.

Mary is as baffled and quietly grateful as we are that God chose her, that he sides with humanity permanently against all who oppose us, even our own hatred of ourselves.

At the end of a long season of bearing, at the end of a long journey, after holding him close to her heart, she stops bearing God for the first time since she said to Gabriel, "Let it be." She lays his bright flesh in a feed trough, swaddled against the anxiety of leaving her womb, nestled by wool and straw from the cold night's sting.

The One who was God before all worlds lies there—as helpless against fragile existence as any of us, bound to the poverty of homelessness, a slave now to the elements he created, a hungering creature of necessity, soon to be a refugee fleeing political terror—held aloft from the damp ground by wood that as God he holds together.

At the dedication of the temple, Solomon said of this tightly wrapped bundle of dust, “Even heaven and the highest heaven cannot contain you” (1 Kings 8:27). Yet contained he was for nine months within this weary teenager, smeared with dirt, sweaty from her labor, catching her breath in time with this baby, the One who in the beginning breathed the stars into the astonished sky above them.

The beginning and end of the Christian revelation of God and God’s love for us, of all Jesus does for us and for our salvation, is this baby, this mother, this dust, this sweat, the wood of this feed trough (and the wood that is to come), their halting, fragile breaths.

God takes the form of a baby because divine *helplessness* is greater than any other force in the universe.

Now, what it is to be human is forever bound up in what it is for one human to be God, born of this woman. Our common humanity can never again sink lower than the throne in which our human brother now sits, still bearing the flesh Mary gave him.

As glorious as all of this is, it was dangerous for God to become human, and it remains dangerous for any human to become human as God is human in the world we humans have made of the world God created. We ponder the wonder of Christmas by resisting the evil that Christmas opposes.

DRAGON

The story of the world—the world's true story from which all true stories are told—happens in a world exactly like our world.

It was a world of emperors and governors; of trade routes and ships; of armies and missiles; of wheat, wine, and oil; of well-appointed houses and crowded tenements; of swords and spears; of inns and caves and lean-tos; of banquets and famines; of night, stars, cold, and sheep . . . the same world.

And in it, a familiar story plays out. A ruler feared and storied, a man regarded as a god, Caesar Augustus, whose name means "exalted one," wants a head count of his conquered masses. By imperial decree, he requires everyone to report to their own towns to be registered.

The government order causes hardship for many. The poor are made to travel long distances on meager resources to the place of their birth for the census, because that's what Caesar's order dictates.

The world's truest story is the story of one such family, a pregnant mother and her rough-handed carpenter fiancé who find no room out in all that cold and all that dark for the God she bears and the God he protects.

The couple makes room for God, all the room God needs: Mary says yes to the divine invitation to bear God in her womb; Joseph heeds the angel and shields Mary, his betrothed, loves her as he has been loved.

Joseph and Mary make room for God, but the world has no room for them because it has no room for God (the surest proof that theirs is the same world as ours) even though she is pregnant and in labor. Such is God's way in this world, homeless and with no place to lay his head.

The first Christians tell us that the couple finds space with the animals in a cave among excrement and straw. And then she gives birth like all mothers do: There are sweat and serum, a cord to cut, and a cry from the human God that splits their ears and their silent night.

Mary wraps his glistening flesh in bands, then lays him in a feed box because, of course, he has come down from heaven to be our true bread, a manna that meets our hunger for love and grants all who eat permanence.

In nearby fields, shepherds are at their late-night watch, awake and alert among the resting sheep. Suddenly the skies above them become a theater. An "angel of the Lord" appears, and the divine glory illumines the hills and the ground beneath their feet like day and envelops them in uncreated light. This isn't the light of the sun or stars. They have never seen this light before, a light from heaven—and they are terrified.

They hear the words that pierce the darkness inside them, words that invisibly shine in every dark moment of the world before and since—and that is *a whole lot* of darkness: "Do not be afraid."

This is the message that God has for all of us and the rest of his beloved creation: Do not be afraid. Today God is born for us, and this is good news of great joy for everyone.

No matter how bad it gets (and it gets pretty bad sometimes), we do not need to be afraid because God has not left us alone.

God becomes what God loves and now lives in the world as one of us, helpless and suffering with us as one of us in a world gone wrong.

The angel tells the shepherds of a sign that accompanies the good news. The sign is familiar to them—a manger—but it is also unexpected and strange: a babe lying in it, wrapped in bands, like the ones they use to prepare bodies for burial.

This is the message that God has for all of us and the rest of his beloved creation: Do not be afraid.

A wondrous hymn from eternity follows as angel song fills the night from countless angels that suddenly appear everywhere, a song composed by the angels for this moment. The hillside and all the earth and all her nations become a great sanctuary for the beauty of the Lord. And their song of exaltation is a transfiguring message: This vulnerable infant is among us as a divine promise that peace is the end of the world's story—not destruction.

The world ends not with a bang or a whimper but with shalom, a well-being that works its slow, patient way into everything. God has made the world so firm that it cannot be moved. This is what humans can now trust about the world even when all hell is set loose.

If it has not all become well, then it is not the end, because the end revealed by this fragile God of clay and breath is the best end imaginable: God in forever union with us and all that in love he makes.

Then as suddenly as they appear, the angels depart with the glory and the uncreated light and the song, and the shepherds are alone again in the dark. With haste they run to see what God has done. And they find the baby just as the angel had said: wrapped in bands and lying in a feed trough.

And if they could see it, for this part is yet hidden from them (and everybody else), there among the animals and the stink, this weary, vigilant mother is clothed with the sun, and the moon is under her feet, and a crown of twelve stars adorns her head.

This is how the Apocalypse describes the nativity of Jesus.

The Revelator sees what the shepherds at the time cannot, not yet. Out in all that dark and all that cold, as Jesus lies immobilized in the feed box, a dragon is roused, awakened by the audacity of a God who becomes vulnerable. The dragon, the thief who deceives and steals and kills—the destroyer—is angry and homicidal.

When the magi arrive a few years later, the dragon appears in Herod, who murders all the young boys born at the same time as Jesus, children who die for God before God dies for them. What the powers did not know is that in killing these children (and eventually killing Jesus), they robbed all violent actions of their permanence. Violence has no future, because of this infant God already shadowed by the cross.

These children and all who suffer violence now have in Jesus Christ a glorious way to endure beyond suffering and death, to shine forever in the kingdom of their Father, while the kingdoms of darkness and their violence await shameful expiration.

The Love that is God never fails, but not because love always triumphs in the ways we are accustomed to expect. In the world as it now is, love's patient victories often fall on either the near or the far side of horrific defeats.

Still, the dragon is as powerless to stop the weakness of God from conquering death as any of the powers that bare their ugly teeth at God's creatures and God's creation—decay, disease, famine, war, hell, and all evil are defeated by the One who suffers with us so that his creation might receive his permanence.

> For a child has been born for us,
>   a son given to us;

> authority rests upon his shoulders;
> and he is named
> Wonderful Counselor, Mighty God,
> Everlasting Father, Prince of Peace.
> Great will be his authority,
> and there shall be endless peace
> for the throne of David and his kingdom.
> He will establish and uphold it
> with justice and with righteousness
> from this time onward and forevermore.
> The zeal of the LORD of hosts will do this. (Isa. 9:6–7)

If we have apocalyptic eyes, we see the "authority that rests on his shoulders" as the cross. The government that rests on the shoulders of the Prince of Peace is not coercion but surrender.

The zeal of the Lord *has done it* by this child. Christmas is believing that God has done it. From the moment the virgin consents to the invitation of God, the head of the dragon is underfoot. Trust that God will rescue us from every horror and banality is the essence of Christian hope. The zeal of the Lord of hosts is always making the world he wants out of the world that is fallen from love.

The zeal is that God is human. The zeal is that the human God loves what he makes and becomes what he loves. The zeal is that God keeps his promises. Jason Micheli says the zeal of the Lord is that "there is no other God but the God who has determined himself not to be God without you."[1]

Forty days after Jesus is born, Mary and Joseph take him to the temple to dedicate him to God, and Anna and Simeon are there, representing a new Eve and Adam.

Unlike the first humans, Anna and Simeon appear in the open without shame. Happy to dwell in the courts of the Lord always, these two humans speak for God about the salvation of the whole world, having waited for the consolation of Israel and the redemption of Jerusalem.

We stand with these ancient ones, and with Mary and Joseph, who from their poverty offer two pigeons and a dove for the consecration of their child and our child. We stand with all the company of heaven and all the angels, and with them we are witnesses to a revelatory moment: God descends to his temple in this infant—an ark you can take into your hands and live, the first ark to be present in the temple in six hundred years, an ark that can never be lost or taken away from humanity.

This child saves us. And at his name every knee shall bow and every tongue confess that this Son of God is Lord to the glory of God the Father (Phil. 2:10–11). We do this the only way anyone can: by the Spirit. We bow the knee and make this confession without coercion because God's love alone is credible.

We do not have to be afraid any longer. Like the shepherds, we can trust the glad tidings of the angels. We are entrusted with the good news that the end is peace, no matter how alone or sad or hurt or alienated we might feel at Christmas.

The poverty of this infant discloses something to us about God: He does not own things or hold power over things as the world does or expects. He holds all things in breath and movement—and we can depend on that—but this tiny sovereign bestows all things in humility, generosity, and freedom.

Pope Francis helps us grasp this more deeply: "One who embraces the universe needs to be held in another's arms. The One who created the sun needs to be warmed. Tenderness incarnate needs to be coddled. Infinite love has a miniscule heart that beats softly. . . . The Bread of life needs to be nourished. The Creator of the world has no home. Today, all is turned upside down: God comes into the world in littleness. His grandeur appears in *littleness*."[2]

When we encounter the smallness of this human child, his neediness and frailty, we must remember it is an unveiling of God, not an obscuring. God is not becoming something that God is not but revealing to us what it means to be the hidden God from eternity.

His poverty is, as Paul says, not a lack but a fullness, an indescribable gift, overflowing in abundance (2 Cor. 8:9). Divine poverty is what holds all things together, sets all things in motion, gives life and light, divine energy and spirit to all living things. His perfect love casts out fear.

"Do not be afraid," the angels tell us still. This gospel is good news for everyone because God is revealed as one of us, who is with us and for us—the human for all humans in whom all humans have light.

This light that enlightens all people is content to go unnoticed in the world, to live among us without fanfare. It turns out that hiddenness is what it means to be God living a human life, what it means for God to be human in eternity, and so also what it means for us to become human as God is human.

HIDDEN

The incarnation means God gets sawdust in his eyes and dirt under his fingernails.

Jesus sets to work with his carpenter stepfather, crafting with Joseph ordinary household things from the same materials that he, as the Word from before all ages, spoke into being.

Jesus spends decades in obscurity, hidden, as most humans are—working and living and celebrating and suffering in anonymity and silence. This is the way it is with God. Like the best waiters at table, Jesus does not draw attention to himself even as he takes care of so very many things without us noticing.

We know next to nothing about the hidden early life of Jesus in Egypt and Galilee. We do know that he was first a child and then a young man. Irenaeus says that Jesus lives every stage of human development: He submits to infancy to hallow the lives of children (*Against Heresies* 2.22.4). Then by his experiences as a teenager, he makes adolescence sacred—those halting, sometimes awkward years when we are no longer a child but not quite an adult. And he survives all that struggle into what was at the time middle age to sanctify growing old.

When God takes on flesh, he does not despise any aspect of what it means to be human. This includes the hardships of being a child, the loneliness and isolation he must have felt in his village, where rumor says he is illegitimate. His family and those close to him do not know him as he knows or comes to know himself, as the Son of God.

This sense of being alone among all his human brothers and sisters, a treasure hidden in the field of the world, drew the Son of God into lonesome places apart, into the company of his Father.

Luke gives us a glimpse into Christ's decades of hiddenness and prayer. After his family's annual Passover pilgrimage to Jerusalem, Jesus stays behind in the city to be a child in the temple with his Father.

The caravan gets a day's journey out when Mary and Joseph discover that Jesus is missing among his family and friends. They rush back only to search the city for days before finding him huddled with the teachers of Israel, listening to them and in his turn asking questions, inviting us all into a conversation with God about the meaning of existence.

As a child, he asks them (and us) what he later asks others: "What is written in the law? How do you read it?" We are stunned that God invites us into a conversation about what it all means. God wants to know how we read.

Jesus tells the elders of Israel great and hidden things, things that were concealed but in the last days revealed, because in him are hidden all wisdom and knowledge, but they and his parents still don't see him for who he is. The elders are astounded by his answers, just as later many mouths are shut by what he says about the law in his great sermon on the mountain.

Dietrich Bonhoeffer writes that Christ's hidden life in the world, like leaven in bread, like a dead seed planted in the ground, is remaking the world so that what should be impossible is becoming possible, so that turning the other cheek and loving our enemies heal the world: "The words [of the sermon] are divine commandments for our action in history insofar as they are the reality of history that has been fulfilled in Christ. They are words that in and through Christ have been implanted [*eingesenkt*] into history; they are its hidden life, which is visible [in] Christ alone."[1]

The benedictions with which Jesus begins his great sermon (Matt. 5:3–11) tell us that we must become like children: poor, powerless, dependent, vulnerable, mistreated, ignored, often misunderstood and maligned while still seeing the world and those around us with fresh, pure, merciful eyes. We must learn to see as those whose vision isn't yet clouded by cynicism and world-weariness, with the humility and defenselessness of love.

At the very onset of Mark's Gospel, the adult Jesus arrives at the house of Peter and Andrew, and no one knows that the carpenter and miracle worker who enters this seaside village is also the Maker of the ends of the earth. As word gets out, the broken humans who begin to gather at the fishermen's house, arriving weary and heavy-laden, are clueless about this One who gives them rest. Jesus's identity as God-with-us is invisible.

Jesus takes the hand of Peter's mother-in-law in his own hand—the hand that set the stars in the vault of heaven, the hand that will be pierced by nails, the hand of love—and raises her from a bed of fever and death by the holy fire of humility that he is, the One who consumes her fever and heals and revitalizes her body. She prepares supper for Jesus and his followers, and Jesus breaks and blesses the bread at table.

And after the healing and after the meal, it is no longer the brothers' door at which the outcasts and refugees gather but the door of Jesus. Into the long post-Sabbath night, by candlelight and by the uncreated light of the Father that shines from his face, he makes bodies well, renews minds, and frees spirits, and one by one everyone heads home, new creations in a creation slowly, patiently being made new.

Tired from a Sabbath of working, Jesus finally rests, and here the story enters the beauty of holiness: The human God gets up in the middle of night, journeys to a lonely place, and prays.

Capernaum rests on hills that rise from the shore of Galilee. Jesus, a cloaked and anonymous figure, walks up into the wooded hills, past the last cul-de-sacs and alleyways of the village, out into the sacred darkness.

The spirits of evil watch him. They know who he is and cower. The creation knows this One too. The ground beneath his feet rejoices, and the trees of the field clap their hands. He travels in silence, but all creation, in which his glory is hidden—the stars and the birds and all else—recognizes the Alpha and the Omega and sings.

He is afflicted with what he has seen of human suffering, and as he walks in solitude, he prays. God prays! I wonder what sort of prayers God prays.

Humans are made in the image of a God who prays. So part of what it means to be human is not only to die but also to pray—to pray in secret, to pray alone, to pray cruciform prayers.

In the morning, the disciples search for Jesus and find him in prayer. They tell him, "Everyone is looking for you." (This may be the truest thing the disciples ever say.) Jesus has waited on the Lord and his strength is renewed. He is prepared by prayer to heal the sick, open the eyes of the blind, free the chained, and cast out evil. He is prepared for this labor by his transparency to his Father.

We need not hide ourselves from him as the humans that we are. Jesus shows us the way to be human as God is human. In his unique person, he reveals aspects of human life we sometimes wrongly consider transgressive—anxiety, feelings of abandonment, struggles with uncertainty, strong emotions like anger and sorrow—as capable of sinlessness. Jesus shows us that humans can be an amalgam of trust and uncertainty. We can be anxious about suffering, mournful and brooding about the state of the world and our sometimes-desperate life in it. We can be hurt by betrayals, made angry about injustice, and so many things Jesus is without doing harm to our communion with God or each other.

Jesus has skin in the game of being human. And not everything we label sin is sin; some of it is just the outworkings of being desperately human in a chaotic, alarming world. Life is a cross, and human responses to hardship, oppression, and the brokenness of creation are part of what it means for God to be human and part of what it means that we humans participate by grace in the divine image. We rejoice that he took on himself our actual circumstances and contingencies in a fallen world to heal all that afflicts life with death, light with false darkness, sacred darkness with false light, joy with grief, wellness with pain, goodness with evil.

Jesus has skin in the game of being human.

A Jewish tradition teaches that about thirty-six righteous persons in every generation of humans behold the divine presence every day. As the belief goes, their quiet ministrations are the reason the world continues to exist.

If you went looking for them, you could not find them. They might have been cobblers, water bearers, or chimney sweeps in older times, orderlies, plumbers, or bus drivers in ours—unnoticed laborers who emerge only when the world is in trouble.

They are persons who live hidden lives, doing unnoticed things. This tradition ennobles all the people no one sees who do so much for the actual good of the world, who work to stay under the radar.

Jesus stands in this tradition. When Jesus does great good things for others, he often asks them to keep it a secret, to tell no one. Some speculate this is because he does not want to draw attention to himself until it's time for his divine nature to be revealed. But it seems to me that the whole of his life among us is hidden because that is simply the sort of human, the sort of God, Jesus is.

By grace, we join the human God in being human as he is human. Our alms are hidden, our prayers are hidden, our fasting is hidden—all done in secret because we join the anonymity of God. The life of all who share the human nature Christ assumes is hidden with Christ in God.

We find our face and we find our name in Jesus Christ—who always emerges from silence and the wilderness to overcome the darkness with light, to release the prisoners, to heal the broken-hearted, to defeat death by death, to become human by refusing to grasp for equality with God, to become human by being nailed to a tree, to become human by entering hell, to become human by drawing very near to the real possibility of being swallowed up by nonexistence in full trust that Love is stronger than death, to become human by a sacred experience we call resurrection, to know from the inside that embodied life is eternal, that the graveyards we fill with the dead by our violence and Word-less words are not the last word but the next to last.

Once when I was alone, I had a sense of being bounded by a vast Mystery that makes itself small, and my words are useless to say more about that moment, but somehow this Mystery, the human God, has united himself to us and to all things because Love loves us until we become what Love is.

What Jesus Christ reveals about the Creator, about what it means to be human, about the meaning of existence, about the love that holds the world in place is so beautiful and so vast. Christ is so radiant and good. The human God has no need to be seen or to lord anything over us. Love seeks only to love us by putting all humans before himself.

Theology can be tempted by swagger and exultation. We forget that only humility can see God or bear witness to God's glory.

When God is humility and hiddenness, only humility and hiddenness can make God known.

At the start of John's Gospel, some priests arrive to ask John the Baptist who he is. He denies being the Christ, being Elijah. He even denies being a prophet, but is there a better description of a genuine vocation in prophecy than his answer: "I am the voice of one crying out in the wilderness" (John 1:23)?

All the prophets of history are named in this reply: alone, howling into empty space, voices echoing off stone, heeded by no one.

But what moves me are the words that follow: "Among you stands one whom you do not know, the one who is coming after me; I am not worthy to untie the strap of his sandal" (John 1:26–27).

I imagine John, the crowds gathered for baptism, and John's questioners standing together on the banks of the Jordan near Bethany. They are in Judaea. The One of whom John speaks is in Galilee.

I picture Jesus, planing one last door, brushing the shavings off his arms—himself the portal, the door between, to and from all things—at labor like any other human, working for decades in obscurity, wiping sweat from his brow, setting doors on hinges, himself the cardinal point of history.

His anonymity is simply God revealed in a human life. His obscurity is simply the divine life, always and everywhere invisibly serving, a love that does not boast, that is not self-seeking. As Bonhoeffer reminds us, "The genuine work of love is always a hidden work. . . . Genuine love is always self-forgetful."[2]

BAPTISM

Walk with me down a dusty path to the Jordan River. Jesus stands among the tall reeds on the bank, having just arrived from Nazareth.

He wades in the water ankle deep. The cool, flowing water soothes his tired, dirty feet. Jesus watches his brothers and sisters descend one by one, entering the water to be cleansed, to repent, drawing near to the formidable presence of the Baptizer.

Dietrich Bonhoeffer says that Jesus "does not want to be considered the only perfect one at the expense of [his fellow humans]."[1] Rather, he expresses solidarity with everyone gathered to be made well, to amend their ways, by—what wondrous love is this?—presenting himself for baptism too.

As Jesus approaches John, the Baptist recognizes not just his cousin, with whom he played as a child, but Isaiah's lamb, the One who takes away the sin of the world. John balks. He is reluctant to do what Jesus asks of him. He can't see why Jesus would submit to a rite of repentance. He balks because he can't see the cross reflected in the waters. He does not understand that Jesus is already here in the murky flow of the Jordan, descending into chaos, shadow, and death, taking on himself the sin of the whole world in order to bear it away.

Jesus, as God, does not remain on the banks of the river, uninvolved and untouched, aloof from the sootiness and flux of our existence. No, he joins us in our predicament, participates without sin in our highs and lows, remains with us always, especially in the moment of our death, including all the preparatory deaths each of us suffers—some everyday and predictable, some unexpected and unbearable—along the way to our last end, an end that he has already suffered and claimed as his own.

Jesus is baptized to be in intimate solidarity with every human. His baptism does not separate Jesus from humans but draws every human into the triune fellowship of Love.

Unlike the children of Israel who walk across on dry land, Jesus goes down under the water to be with the armies of Pharaoh and with those taken by the great flood. The human God stands squarely with humanity, rejects all human and demonic contempt for humankind, identifies himself with our worst crimes, surrenders his perfections that all might participate in his divine goodness, stands in our place as the representative of all that is truly human.

Our God is a *baptized* God. He identifies with all so that he might identify all with himself. In Christ, he has made it so that what happens to him happens to us and what happens to us happens to him. Jesus wants us to be human as God is human.

And Jesus doesn't remain in this tomb of water; he rises. And he doesn't rise alone. As he comes up out of the chaos of the flood, he brings Adam and Eve and all their sons and daughters with him from the depths.

Rising, he prays. And his prayers rise to heaven. What does he pray? "Father, forgive them"? "Father, make them one"? "Father, pour out your Spirit on all flesh"? He prays all these prayers and more.

Jesus's prayers open the heavens. As he emerges from the dark, cool waters, his heart aflame with prayer, there is something that can only be described as the sound of wings, a flash of feathers. The Holy Spirit, who spoke through the prophets, alights on him in the body of a dove.

We are told that at this moment the sky is torn—we might say a window or a portal opens in space-time—and through the tear in the fabric of existence, a voice speaks: "You are my Son, the Beloved; with you I am well pleased" (Mark 1:11).

The majestic voice proceeds from the invisible Father who dwells in light so bright no one can approach him. Yet here the Father is near to his Son, and so to us, not "out there" in some distant space but here, now, present in and to what is happening.

The Spirit too is near, revealed by the form of this dove descending. In this riverside moment when the Son draws near to every human who has ever lived or ever will live, the Father is made audible by the Spirit, and the Spirit is made visible by the Father. Ponder this with me a moment longer.

God is not soliloquy but conversation, not solo but chorus, not alone but a harmony of crucified Love without origin or end. The Spirit rests on the Son, the Son rests in the bosom of the Father, and the creation enters its rest with us, invited by the One who is gentle and humble of heart: "Come to me, all you who are weary and are carrying heavy burdens, and I will give you rest" (Matt. 11:28).

Christ's baptism anticipates Christ's transfiguration on Tabor's heights and his crucifixion outside Jerusalem's walls. In all these, all of God is present in the Son's solidarity with us in our mortality. We see that the Son is never without his Father, who is always too near to be seen, and that the Son's life is a life saturated with and impelled by the Spirit, who is seen so the Father can be heard.

Tellingly, Mark's account of the crucifixion (15:37–39) mirrors Jesus's baptism (1:10–11): Jesus breathes his last (expiring the Spirit, inspiring all things), the veil of the temple tears (the same verb used about the sky in 1:10), and the centurion, who sees how

Jesus dies, who has seen many die by crucifixion, somehow sees something more, something beyond the everyday crucifixion—sees the Father *because* he sees the Son—and confesses, "Truly this man was God's Son" (15:39).

Baptism and crucifixion, we see, go together. And those who are baptized into Jesus's death also share in his resurrection (Rom. 6:3–4), an eternal share in his triune life with the Father and the Spirit.

We need no analogies, no geometry, to explain the Trinity. The Trinity is not solvable math but unfathomable mystery. Instead of mentally grasping the mystery, we are immersed in the triune life by the power of the Spirit. The Trinity is also known by saying the names Father, Son, and Holy Spirit as we make the sign of the cross on our bodies, as many do in the liturgical church traditions.

Making the sign of the cross comes to us from the first Christians. It was so common among them that Tertullian says they wore out their foreheads signing themselves.[2] Basil of Caesarea lists it *first* among other embodied practices like facing east in prayer and anointing the baptized with oil (*On the Holy Spirit* 27.66).

Anyone can bring their thumb, forefinger, and middle finger together as a sign of the triune life—Father, Son, and Spirit. And they can bring their ring and small finger together as a sign that Jesus is at once divine and human—that all he is and says and does is what God is and what humanity is. Resting these last two fingers in the palm of the hand is a sign that the Son descends into our world to rescue us from death.

The Trinity is not solvable math but unfathomable mystery.

Move the gathering of your thumb and forefingers upward to touch your forehead, then move this gathering of fingers straight down to touch your sternum (some go lower, to the navel), then move them across your heart to touch your left shoulder, and finally move them across your chest to touch your right shoulder. That is the gesture.

In the Terrence Malick film *A Hidden Life*, the Austrian villagers take the tips of their thumbs only and sign a cross on their foreheads, on their lips, and finally on their hearts, as many do before the Gospel passage is read in church.

The triune Love, who are together one God, is not a puzzle we solve or a problem we graph but a witnessed mystery we *enter*, a witnessed mystery that transfigures us. The triune Love attunes us to God, to one another, and to ourselves, illuminating us both from without and from within with the light that is our life.

We see the Son standing in living water beloved by his Father and empowered by the Spirit. God loves the world so much that he sends this Son not to condemn the world but to save the world through him. Seeing Jesus Christ, we recognize ourselves for the first time.

We are invited to be human as God is human. And here is wisdom: The invitation is in front of us in every moment as a divine gift. And divine invitations carry with them the ability to say yes to them.

Jesus is not an example of the kind of life we could live if only we knew the secret. His life becomes ours for the living. His love becomes ours for the loving. It is all divine gift.

God means to make us his equals. We are not Christ's servants but his friends, his bride, his body. We are not his slaves but his co-heirs. Everything, truly everything the Father means for the Son is intended also for us by the Spirit. We can love others as the human God loves us.

TEMPTATION

After descending into the dark waters of baptism, Jesus enters the wilderness of beauty and silence, of parched and shivering extremes, of hunger and sorrow, of terror and shadow, of life and death. He is driven by the Spirit to every limitation, where the companions of the human God are jackals and ravens.

Jesus fasts for forty days with all who hunger, with those who starve when we believe the lie that there is not enough for all of us, when we believe that the world is founded on scarcity instead of abundance. His nourishment is prayer, his hidden manna the Father's will.

The new Adam keeps a fast when the old Adam (and Eve) could not, when his ancestors who were delivered from Egypt could not, when we cannot, so that now we, they, and everyone can.

Then something less than a person but more than a metaphor appears, more shadow than substance, a father of lies—the Accuser.

Chromatius, a fifth-century bishop, imagines that satan has been watching Jesus with increasing curiosity:

> He [satan] heard that it had been announced by the angel to the Virgin that she would give birth to the Son of God. . . . He saw,

> after the baptism, the Holy Spirit descending like a dove. He also heard the Father's voice from heaven saying, "This is my Son."
>
> He heard John with a loud voice proclaiming, "This is he who takes away the sin of the world." Disturbed by so much testimony therefore and now troubled by this voice, this is what he feared most of all: that after he had filled the world with sins, he heard there would now come someone to take away the sins of the world.[1]

At the end of Jesus's fast, it's his hunger that the devil seeks to exploit, not understanding that hunger is, for the human God, strength.

Satan says to Jesus, "If you are the Son of God, command these stones to become loaves of bread" (Matt. 4:3). With this statement, the devil is trying to sort out if Jesus is divine or human, unaware that Jesus is their perfect union. Satan tempts Jesus to leave the limits of ordinary existence, to do magic tricks, to defy nature, and to prove in those ways that he is what satan suspects he might be: a god.

Satan could not imagine that remaining human, accepting limitations, binding oneself in humility to created boundaries is the sacred vocation of all humans because it is the way Christ our God is human.

Many of the first Christians, starting with Origen of Alexandria (*On First Principles* 2.6.6), talk about how an iron knife is known by certain properties (it is cold, hard, sharp), but when it is set in flame, it is known no longer by the properties of iron but by the properties of fire (it is hot, malleable, searing). Likewise, in hunger and weakness Jesus is known by the properties of flesh, but as satan tests his faithfulness, these things—hunger and weakness—are in Jesus revealed to be human *and divine*, humanly divine and divinely human. Jesus's flesh is known by the properties of the Spirit's fire.

Jesus refuses to make stones into bread, replying: "One does not live by bread alone, but by every word that comes from the mouth of God" (Matt. 4:4). None of us can make bread from rocks, and Jesus is one of us in all the limitations humans share. While for us limitations are frustrations, for Jesus they are freedoms. Knowing that, we begin to understand that when Jesus remains human in his exchanges with the devil, he also remains divine. For Jesus Christ to stop being human is to stop being God, and to stop being God is to stop being human. In him, they are always one and the same.

We have trouble accepting this, because we have been taught to think of divinity as an abstraction, defined by its difference from us. As a result, we often think of the incarnation as a humiliation for God, an embarrassment, if not an outright absurdity, when for God it is an honor to be human.

After all, the Son of God is not becoming something God is not when he becomes human ("Let us make humans in *our image*" Gen. 1:26), and the Son of God does not lay aside or hide what it means to be God when he becomes one of us.

Likewise, humans do not become something we are not when we become human as God is revealed to be human in Jesus Christ. Jesus is not himself apart from us and we are not ourselves apart from him.

We often think of the incarnation as a humiliation for God, an embarrassment, if not an outright absurdity, when for God it is an honor to be human.

Christ is the image of the Father, and the image in which all humans are made, so what it means to be human is unknown until the Son appears and makes it known (Irenaeus, *Against Heresies* 5.16.2). Imitation of the Son's humanity is *how* by grace we become divine as the Son is divine. As Athanasius says, "He was humanized that we might be divinized."[2]

Jesus's most human moments are also his most divine. The humanity he lives does not come at the price of his refusal to be God but is the essence of what it means to be God from eternity.

Here is how George MacDonald articulates it:

> The Father said, That is a stone. The Son would not say, That is a loaf. No one creative fiat shall contradict another. The Father and the Son are of one mind. The Lord could hunger, could starve, but would not change into another thing what His Father had made one thing. There was no such change in the feeding of the multitudes. The fish and the bread were fish and bread before. . . . There was in these miracles, I think in all, only a hastening of appearances: the doing of that in a day, which may ordinarily take a thousand years, for with God time is not what it is with us. . . . Indeed, the wonder of the growing corn is to me greater than the wonder of feeding the thousands. It is easier to understand the creative power going forth at once—immediately—than through the countless, the lovely, the seemingly forsaken wonders of the cornfield.[3]

A miracle may *transform* one thing into another, but it never *deforms* a thing by undoing or abusing its integrity. The Son of God was disfigured by what we did to him. But he, in his goodness, never disfigures us or anything his Father has made. He only ever transfigures, so that by the uncreated light of heaven that radiates from Jesus we see all persons, things, and places as God intends and sees them. And these transfigurations always establish, never efface, our creaturely integrity.

Jesus Christ is both the bread of life and the stone the builders rejected, so he can make bread stones for us and stones bread, but only in ways consistent with his person.

We might ask: Did not the stones the accusers dropped become the bread of life for them and for the woman they wanted to execute? Did not the stone tablets of the law become bread for us in the hands of Christ? Yes. He is bread to all things—sustaining them. He is stone to all things—upholding them. And he can make bread stones and stones bread in ways that do no evil to anyone or anything.

It is not a violation of the created integrity of water to make it wine, or of the nature of water to walk upon it—after all, only the deepest humility can walk on water—and walking on water serves the vocation of reaching and serving the apostles, as turning water to wine serves the wedding guests.

These things are good because they are not violations of what it means to be God (Jesus and the Father are one) or of what it means to be human (humans are in Jesus one with the Father).

Knowing all that, we know why the devil's temptation to turn stones to bread has no purchase on Jesus: He has an infinitely better way of doing it already in mind. He likes the stones in the wilderness as they are. He has other stones in mind, his own flesh and bones, and he makes them bread for us. It is what is written in the flesh of Jesus, the will of God once engraved in stone, that is our bread. This, as Moses said, is what God has given us to eat (Exod. 16:15). His body is our manna.

Jesus is the Word and, as such, every word that proceeds from God's mouth. Christ's are the words that give us life. He makes bread into more bread, gathering all the fragments left over from divine abundance so that there is no scarcity. Humility, patience, and long-suffering—not demonstrations of "power"—are the aromas of this bread. The Son of God becomes flesh not to show us that he is "a god" but to be God with us in our poverties—satan and his pretensions be damned.

Jesus won't perform magic tricks, but satan will. He transports Jesus to the pinnacle of the temple in Jerusalem. The One whose glory once filled this house now stands on its roof in desert-dusty feet. Here satan tempts Jesus again, saying "throw yourself down" (Matt. 4:6), wanting to see if Jesus is God by a rescue of angels, by some demonstration of divine mastery over gravity.

The taunts of satan, using the words of Scripture, are in his mouth no longer the Word of God but something sinister, a blasphemy, for there is already a "throwing down" that makes the cosmos. The foundation of the world—from the Greek, its "throwing down"—is the death of God on the cross (Rev. 13:8). Jesus knows where and when he is to be "thrown down" for the life of the world, knows that cross-shaped love makes the good we call gravity together with all the governing forces of the universe.

Jesus shows us that matter matters. His love is why and how the earth rotates and gravity pulls us down. These forces belong to the Son, are expressions of his love, are part of who the Son is as human and divine. Jesus would no more violate them than strike someone down with a sword.

Jesus trusts that the Father knows all he needs even before he knows he needs it. He does not need a sign of the Father's love for him. He already knows that he is in every moment upheld by the Father. Whatever the Father does or does not do, Jesus knows that the Father has him in all things.

The only sign Jesus will show satan is the sign of Jonah, his own surrender to death and the grave, confident the Father will arrest his fall but not until after he is dead. His response of trust is now the trust available to all humans. In living within the limits of our poverties, Jesus makes them saving. He chooses for us who cannot choose—so we can choose well.

Jesus chooses powerlessness and lack and gratitude, which turn out to be the ground of all comfort, provision, and rest. As Malcolm Guite says, "Jesus . . . shows his solidarity once and for all with all of us, trusting himself to our flesh and blood so that we can trust our flesh and blood to him."[4] Being tempted in every way as we are, he is the One who responds well for all of us in all our temptations. What he does is done in such a way that our doing of it is made possible.

We will at a later point reflect on the last temptation, but here we raise full-throated hallelujahs to Christ in his victory in the wilderness. Satan dared to offer Jesus the kingdoms of the world when in fact the world itself—the whole creation—belongs to him eternally.

We delight in seeing that Jesus does not fall for such a silly trick, but we also sorrow, sobered by knowing that his victory in this moment anticipates the dark events a few short years hence, of the coming sacred week that once for all saves the world.

If the early life of Jesus is, for the most part, quiet and unseen, his three years of public ministry are simply that same humility made audible and visible. In the chapters that follow, we will ponder the sort of human life God lives so we too might in his Spirit live the same vulnerability.

A HUMAN LIFE

Jesus, the human face of God and the divine face of [humanity].

—John Paul II, *Angelus*, January 11, 2004

Christ is the anti-hero of the gods: bearer of troubling promises, ever reluctant to display power. Christ is hard to follow, because we desire pleasure and power, and he is not offering us any. We hoped God was a god. But he is not. He is God. What he offers is himself, and for many of us, that is the greatest disappointment of all.

—Andy Squyres, *Poet Priest*, vol. 2

Perhaps Christ goes to sleep that he may bless sleep also; perhaps he is tired that he may hallow weariness also; perhaps he weeps that he may make tears blessed.

—Gregory of Nazianzen, *Oration* 37

In Christ's incarnation, all of humanity regains the dignity of bearing the image of God. Whoever from now on attacks the least of the people attacks Christ, who took on human form and who in himself has restored the image of God for all who bear a human countenance.

—Dietrich Bonhoeffer, *The Cost of Discipleship*

SYNAGOGUE

For decades of his life, Jesus lives in a small village of perhaps two hundred persons, all of whom would've known Jesus and his family terribly well. Jesus is a fixture in the synagogue of Nazareth, attending every Sabbath, just as Joseph and Mary had taught him.

Many in the congregation know him as a tradesman, a woodworker who hangs doors, who takes care of his young, devout mother. They saw him grow up, playing with other children in the village. They've witnessed him at times of prayer, and they've seen him bent to his labors. One imagines he has been asked to read the Scriptures before, but this time, as the attendant places the scroll of Isaiah in his callused hands, Jesus stands among them as One they do not know.

Jesus unrolls the scroll and reads this: "The Spirit of the Lord is upon me, for he has anointed me to bring Good News to the poor. He has sent me to proclaim that captives will be released, that the blind will see, that the oppressed will be set free, and that the time of the Lord's favor has come" (Luke 4:18–19 NLT).

He rolls up the words of the prophet Isaiah, places the scroll back in the attendant's hands, and sits down. And every eye in the place is on him. If he had read the Scriptures before, he had not read them like *that*. Then in the anointed silence he begins to preach, saying, "The Scripture you've just heard has been fulfilled this very day!" (Luke 4:21 NLT). His proclamation leaves them speechless, pressed toward prayer and praise.

Luke reports that they are amazed by the sermon, cannot believe that the son of Joseph has it in him. His words are full of grace and life, like a lantern in a dark place, like honey in the mouth.

This carpenter's eloquence is nothing new. He'd recently become renowned throughout Galilee as a preacher. Should the Nazarenes not have known this? Did the Spirit hide his graces from them? Or did they turn their faces away? Are they scandalized by Jesus and what he says? Or are they scandalized by themselves and their own lack of awareness and understanding?

God had made a tent among them in the body of this rabbi, even if his fellow villagers couldn't or wouldn't see this teacher who desired nothing but their healing. The words of Isaiah had taken on flesh in Jesus. His hometown congregation ends up rejecting him when he points out that God feeds and heals even those they despise, but many of the poor and needy of Galilee go on to follow him. In his consecrated and consecrating hands, the Scriptures become bread for the oppressed.

The poor meet the living God in the human ways we meet anyone: an embrace at the door of their home, a brush of his hand as bread is passed, a late-night conversation by a fire. They behold and hear and touch the Word of Life as Jesus puts flesh and bone to the promises of Isaiah: The eyes of the blind are opened; the poor are comforted; prisoners are set free; good news is preached to the oppressed; God's favor arrives. And these encounters with the Word are unapologetically natural, involving the stuff of earth: wood, oil, water, sand, spit, blood, sweat, tears, bread, and wine.

Jesus is the Word of God in the vivid experiences of those who know him in flesh and blood: walking the streets of Capernaum and the alleyways of Jerusalem, fishing at dawn on Galilee, or dining in Bethany. Jesus teaches those who encounter him in the wilderness and seaside villages to see him—a man who eats and drinks with them and sleeps on the ground beside them—as one with the God revealed in the experiences of patriarchs, psalmists, and prophets, as the One who delivered Israel from Egypt and returned the exiles from Babylon.

We can see Jesus now in the words of the Scriptures because others encountered him in the real world and then and only then wrote about those encounters—often long after. Jesus Christ is revealed in and by those to whom he appeared—the witnesses who accompanied the Word of God in animate clay, who, after his cross, came to understand him as the angel, the visitor, and the pillar who appear in the Scriptures of Israel. Jesus shows them how these ancient stories, poems, cries for help, and prophecies were, in the end, all about him.

Here it might be helpful to introduce a Greek word: *anamnēsis*. It means to experience in the present what has happened in the past. When we gather in worship to remember Jesus and the saving events that bring salvation, we do not merely recall events of the past. We *experience* them as present events because of Jesus Christ. As Robert Jenson writes, "Time, as we see it framing biblical narrative, is neither linear nor cyclical but perhaps more like a helix, and what it spirals around is the risen Christ."[1] Every point in time is equidistant from the incarnation, passion, and resurrection of Jesus.

This can be hard to understand, but it's an important part of the Christian mystery of salvation. Every single person who meets Jesus—past, present, and future—is truly met by Christ regardless of their proximity to the first century. Jesus doesn't need to overcome the distinction between the past and the present or the present and the future.

Every time we gather in his name, Jesus brings himself and the wholeness of his being—including every moment of his incarnate life among us—with him. Every moment of play, every moment of rest, as well as every prayer, every task, every kindness—where Christ is, the fullness of life is present, and so the fullness of God.

Jesus Christ is the Word of God present among us as a living person. Or as Brian Zahnd puts it, "God couldn't say all he wanted to say in the form of a book, so he said it in the form of a human life."[2]

Mysteriously, Jesus, living the life he received from Mary, learns from Moses what he himself revealed to Moses on the mountain. Just as he was David's Lord as David's son, and Mary's deliverer as the one delivered by her, he is Moses's teacher as Moses's disciple. The Scriptures are the Word of God, we might say, just in the sense that Jesus, the Word of God, receives them as the truth of his own life given for the sake of the Father's love for the world.

The Scriptures bear testimony to Jesus Christ, the living God, who reveals himself without remainder in the incarnate Son. When in the synagogue we see Jesus, we see the Father, breathing eternal wisdom through Jesus's sun-parched lips by the Spirit.

When in the synagogue we see Jesus, we see the Father, breathing eternal wisdom through Jesus's sun-parched lips by the Spirit.

The only exhaustive Word the Father speaks is Jesus Christ.

Jesus invites us to trust the Scriptures, assured that whatever in its pages seems to be an offense to the God Jesus reveals has a way of being read that doesn't do violence to who Jesus is. As Augustine says, we "turn over in our minds and meditate upon what we read till an interpretation be found that tends to establish the reign of love,"[3] until we can restore every passage of Scripture to its natural position and vitality in the flesh of Jesus.

We know all this because those who first encountered Jesus Christ in this world that he created good, who found him in the manger and beheld him on the cross, wrote down their experiences with the human God. Their remembrances are inspired by the Spirit, beautiful and effective, precisely because they serve a greater reality: They reveal a personal God who transcends the words on the page, the human who is with us always to the end of the world—sacred heart, breath of life, with arms that can embrace us, seated at the Father's right hand until he makes death a footstool.

When the Word walks and talks and laughs and dines with you, you understand that there's a profound difference between the spirit and the letter of Holy Scripture, and that spirit is Jesus Christ. His life among us, and the words of Scripture that illumine that life, are in this world the icon of the Father's endless regard and care for all things.

ICON

On a wall in the chapel of Saint Catherine's Monastery, at the base of Mount Sinai in Egypt, hangs one of the oldest Christian icons. The Sinai *Pantocrator* (Greek for "ruler of all things") is no ordinary icon. No surviving icon of its era looks anything like it. It seems fresh, as if painted yesterday.

Believed to have been given to the monastery in the mid-sixth century by the Byzantine Emperor Justinian, the Pantocrator weathered a period when icons were destroyed in many urban churches. It was preserved in the arid climate of Sinai and was secured from invaders by an order of protection given by the prophet Muhammad, signed with a tracing of his palm print, after the monks of Saint Catherine's gave him shelter and hospitality.

The Christ of Sinai is perhaps the closest thing we have to a photograph of God. It is meant to be for us a divine and human portrait that draws us into mystical communion with the person we behold.

This icon tells the story of Good Friday and Easter, of the singular event of redemption the first Christians called Pascha. Viewers will note the difference between the left side of the face, in which some see evidence of Christ's torture and passion, and the right side, in which some discern his transfigured, resurrected radiance.

The eyes stand out. Something about them seems not quite "right." They have an unsettling quality. The more time I spent in prayer, gazing at this unique image of Jesus, the more the asymmetry of the eyes troubled me. I pondered why the artist would paint Jesus with a physical "imperfection." Eventually, I realized this was not a problem with the artist or the image but rather a limitation of my imagination, a failure to see everything there is to see in Christ.

One of my childhood friends had a lazy eye. More than I would like to admit, I often caught myself staring. I see now that that was a test of my faith, because it brought to light what I did not believe to be true about the Word made flesh (John 1:4), made like us in every respect (Heb. 2:17).

Hard as it is to believe and trust, Jesus took on *everything* it means to be human. Jesus grew tired, donned a cloak against the piercing cold and burning sun, could catch a virus or suffer a wasting disease. And if all that is true, he might also have borne physical "defects." Isaiah's prophecy of the Suffering Servant signals that Jesus has "nothing beautiful or majestic about his appearance, nothing to attract us to him" (53:2b NLT).

I discovered it was not just a matter of accepting that Jesus's face might have a distinguishing "flaw." I had never settled at my contemplative core that the divine became one with matter in Jesus: real flesh, real bones, real heart, wed to "very God of very God."

My encounter with the Sinai Pantocrator helped end my inherited image of Jesus as a stick figure in a Bible story—a Sunday school flannelgraph character—so that I might experience the full-blooded actuality of how things are in Jesus Christ. Icons of Christ help us consider that Jesus is no abstraction—no mere thought, no matter how beautiful; no hero in a children's story told to make us feel better. Rather, he is the express image of the unseen, all-holy God made vulnerable (Col. 1:15), made like us in every way.

The Potter who makes us from clay becomes clay. The Potter takes on the earthen stuff he molds at the invisible wheel of his heart when he makes us. The indestructible becomes destructible.

The Potter is molded in the womb of his fragile mother, and then the clay of his flesh is scored, forever scarred, by decades of life in this world he created and that we damaged, is betrayed and murdered by his brothers, and becomes in the end a "potsherd," a broken fragment of ceramic, dry and without water, nailed to hardwood.

And yet—after descending to the innumerable broken fragments of humanity that lay silent in the grave!—Jesus is made new on the third day by the fire of the Spirit so that all broken vessels might be mended and recast in his unbreakable permanence and beauty, to join him as one human body, one Christ.

Understand how worthy you are made by these actions of God. Understand the measureless Love that formed you and that searches for you like a collector of fine pottery, who binds himself forever to what he has made, for the sake of the Love that he forever is.

The Sinai icon helps us face a reality that cannot be intellectually comprehended: We become most truly human when we embrace the humanity of God in Jesus Christ. Icons help us visualize such an incredible possibility: that we can become transfigured partakers of the divine nature in clay (2 Pet. 1:4).

Fifteen hundred years after its creation, the Sinai Pantocrator still hangs in the shadow of the mountain on which God forbade the worship of idols.

Here, it's worth noting that icons are not idols. Idols are objects *we make* and worship in place of the living God, whereas *God has begotten* a perfect image of himself in the human flesh of Jesus (Heb. 1:3).

God is not a flower or a mountain or a geometric equation or a projected personality like Isis or Apollo or a clay statue or any of the gods we manufacture to bless our violence, underwrite our greed, and license our impulses. If your god gives you leave to hate, harm, or kill any image bearer, you're worshiping an idol or listening to a devil. If the One you worship does not kill, steal, or destroy, if the One you heed loves the world and all things in her, he is an Icon.

When iconographers depict Christ, they are not fashioning a god for themselves but rendering an image of what the Father, Son, and Spirit have tendered in the incarnation of the one God in Jesus Christ.

Jesus can be described and drawn and sculpted. It is not idolatry that God became flesh in Jesus, and it is not idolatry to depict who God is in Jesus and hang these depictions in our homes and houses of worship just like we hang family photos or images of friends or figures who inspire us. We would never think to tear up such images or deface them, because these pictures represent the people we love. No one worships these depictions. Christians do, however, worship a God who clothed himself in clay.

Women and men are made in the image of God, female and male together bearing all that is in God, and so it shouldn't surprise us when our incarnate Lord looks like us. The Sinai icon reminds us that we are one with God and God is one with us.

Ponder with me for a moment the mystery that we enter when we encounter Christ in the Gospels.

When Jesus is on the Sea of Galilee with the disciples, we find the God who made the waves, the wind, and the wood the boat is crafted from—who made everything and holds everything together—tired and asleep in the hold of the ship.

Our first thought is that Jesus, a flesh-and-blood human, needs a nap. But if what we have been saying about Jesus is true, then God is asleep on a boat. The One who neither slumbers nor sleeps, who always watches over Israel, has surrendered to the weariness of having a human body without ceasing to be divine.

When the disciples awaken Jesus and he surveys the situation (and their hearts), he rebukes their fear, and then a human stands up on two feet in a vessel sloshing with lake water, leans against the ropes, and speaks: "Peace! Be still!"

Though there are exclamations, Jesus does not need to shout. Jesus is human like the rest of the disciples, with breathing lungs and a beating heart, sleepy and finding his sea legs. Yet he makes the wind stop gusting and turns the waves to glass with his words. As readers, we think Jesus is God and that this awe-inspiring ability fits his divinity, but Jesus is also flesh, no more special in his biochemistry than anyone else in that boat on a sea gone wild. Jesus was as susceptible to drowning as his friends.

The One who neither slumbers nor sleeps, who always watches over Israel, has surrendered to the weariness of having a human body without ceasing to be divine.

Jesus is human in the real situation of peril with other humans. This God joins us in our waking to anxiety and peril, risks being actually human, but he experiences the storm differently so we can experience it differently.

When we read every story about Jesus with the sort of contemplation that icons allow, we begin to discern that something has happened forever in God and something has happened forever in us because the Son, who breathed the stars into fiery existence and set their courses in the sky, who made the orchid and the hummingbird, humbled himself and was made like us in every way—weary, thirsty, hungry, aching, longing, striving, rejected, marvelous clay that we are—so that we might be human as God is human.

So if our idea about God includes the notion that God can't die, or that God values himself above his creation, or that God can't touch or look upon or be in the presence of sinners, the person we encounter in the Gospels is going to challenge our abstract divinity.

If our ideal human is someone who uses violence to impose his will or who underwrites our tragic way of life by harnessing the powers of this world because the ends justify the means, the person we encounter in the Gospels is going to challenge our ideal humanity.

If we do not see tyranny in Jesus, then we should not see tyranny as divine. If we do not see coercion in Jesus, then we should not see coercion as truly human. Jesus Christ is all there is in God, and he is all that it means to be human. We look to the radical unveiling of what it means to be divine and what it means to be human in this beautiful, unexpected, homeless Galilean.

When Jesus grows tired or thirsty or when he weeps, that is not his "human side" but what it means to be God revealed in a human life, doing human things divinely.

When he turns water into wine or calms seas or raises the dead, that is not his "divine side" but what it means to be human revealed in a divine life, doing divine things humanly.

In all things, at every moment, Jesus is God all in and human all-in. There are not "parts" in him, no "parts" to play. He is simply one person, the union of all that it means to be God and all that it means to be human.

The Sinai icon reminds us that in Jesus Christ, God leaves fingerprints wherever he goes (Jesus is human without measure), that Jesus breathes the spirit of the Father's loving-kindness on all things (Jesus is divine without qualification). His blood, his touch, his stops of breath reconcile the Creator and the clay that as female and male alone in all creation bear the stamp of God.

If we pay attention, every moment of human encounter is not an abstraction but personal and immediate, for we behold the likeness of Jesus in every human. Would that we might behold in all faces the icon of Christ's vulnerability, selflessness, and resurrection in this wild, wonderful world he came to serve.

SERVANT

He doesn't know whom he's invited to dinner, this ruling Pharisee. Reading the story in Luke 14:1–14, we are blessed to know and want him (and everyone else) to know. The angel of the Lord is his visitor—the very same who stayed the sacrificial hand of Abraham and called to Moses from the flames of the yet-living bush and walked with the Hebrew children in the fiery furnace. The One who is God and an *other* within God by whom God is identified, Light from Light.

No more aware than his brother Nicodemus, even less aware than their God-wrestling father Jacob, the ruler has invited the Lord into his house. He is entertaining not an angel in the usual sense but the One the whole company of angels adores.

He has invited Jesus on the Sabbath, possibly to honor him, possibly to learn from him, possibly to test his mettle in front of his inner circle, including his closest family and friends, the elite of his movement, and the town's bigwigs and heavy hitters.

Jesus is glad to be there, but the irony should not be lost on us. The One who sets every table of the world with every kind of food, the One who oxygenates the air, enriches the soil, gives water its life-granting power—his energies granting sunlight its converting capacity to every nutrient-rich plant—is this here-today, gone-tomorrow politician's houseguest.

Not only is Jesus one with the Father, who gives us everything to eat and all that we drink, from water to wine, but Jesus is also the inspiration in the mind and the grit in the muscle of every farmer, shepherd, harvester, truck driver, and grocer by whom we are fed, whether or not we are giving thanks over our bounty or bearing in mind with gratitude all those whose labor feeds us.

Jesus is the shelterer and the grower, the line cook and the master chef, the load-bearing migrant worker and the waiter who makes all things and sustains all things in life. The One who is by nature generous and neighborly, the One whose name is Kindness, the One who makes possible all our hospitality is one among the many guests at the Pharisee's soirée. In this way, even as guest, Jesus is the ruler's host.

I imagine Jesus at the border of the room, near a window perhaps, gazing into the heart of each of these his friends. Humans are predictable, sadly: These people are consumed with their place at the meal. "What does this placement or arrangement say about me? What does it mean for me? How do I make the most of this opportunity?" And even if they feel a prick of shame, they nonetheless want to be honored.

Are we so different? When we arrive at a wedding and see where we have been seated, don't we compare our place to that of the other guests? At a formal dinner or a party where important people have gathered, do we not sometimes resent where the host has seated us? Our questions are the same as those of the Pharisee's guests. We too are afraid that the world is governed by scarcity. We jostle for recognition.

Yet while they are arguing in their hearts about who is the greatest, Jesus, God incognito, stands among them as One who serves, One who waits on those he loves—as he has done from before the beginning. As Humility, he has their number, and ours. He also has our true name.

I imagine Jesus noticing something else too: The ruler has invited all the "right" people and only them—the executives and power brokers, the notables, monied, beautiful, and proud, the swift, the strong.

The ruler has not invited the poor farmers who raised the food and wine he intends to serve at this feast or the laborers who transported it. He has not invited the homeless or the leprous, the sick, the left for dead, or anyone who is a stranger to him. How could he? He assumes that to do so would be to dishonor Jesus, the One he seeks to honor.

My stepfather had unusual practices when we were young. As a newly minted minister, he took the Gospels quite literally. He did startling things all the time, especially on holidays or occasions when many stick to family and close friends, because he took Jesus at his word. He would get in the family car and drive around downtown Orlando, looking for people on the street to bring home to dinner.

One Thanksgiving he brought home a woman who'd lost her job. Once a chef, she was living on the street. At first, we were a little stunned she was standing in our family kitchen.

She taught us how to make a Western omelet on Thanksgiving morning. I still make eggs the way she taught us. Her presence among us was teaching us how to welcome the stranger, to have empathy, to pay attention to everyone, to learn from all.

There in the house I called home, this young preacher, who had been my stepfather for less than a year, brought people off the street, into our comfortable suburban lives. He showed us what it means to share God's abundance with people whose ways are not our ways and whose thoughts are not our thoughts.

He was a risk-taker who taught us to take risks for the gospel. He showed us what it meant to imitate Jesus and how we ought to behave when we gather at the table where Jesus is one of the guests. And Jesus is *always* one of the guests.

Now as then—both the *then* of my childhood and the *then* of Luke's story—the human God comes to our table, meeting us in the most common human experience, sitting down to a meal with guests. And the more room we make, and the more motley the crew we gather, the more at home Jesus is.

Jesus tells us that everyone is invited to the feast of bread and wine he prepares in the presence of our enemies, those "powers" of evil that seek to steal our humanity—disease, famine, violence, death. Jesus extends a special welcome to the ones whom polite society has forgotten and always seats himself in the lowest place, but only after waiting on us all.

This is the truth at the heart of all that Jesus teaches: "Among the heathen it is their kings who lord it over them, and their rulers are given the title of 'benefactors.' But it must not be so with you! Your greatest man must become like a junior and your leader must be a servant. Who is the greater, the man who sits down to dinner or the man who serves him? Obviously, the man who sits down to dinner—yet I am the one who is the servant among you" (Luke 22:25–27 Phillips).

A cup offered to the thirsty, food offered to the hungry, every comfort given to the weary, all visits to the sick and the prisoner and the dying—done in obscurity, without fanfare, without spotlight, without notice—these are more consequential for the world than anything imposed by armies or governments or corporations. When we invite and serve the poor, we are serving God incognito.

Christ appears to us as the least "desirable" of our neighbors. In our rush to make him superhuman and so much higher than us, we blaspheme the manner in which he chooses to reveal himself.

He is the one who tells us to find him in the naked, the prisoner, the hungry, the stranger. And it is beautiful.

Jesus came not to be served but to serve. And that has always been true and always will be. When Jesus tells us that the greatest in the kingdom is the servant of all the persons who are there, he is speaking not of us but of himself, the model of love. He is speaking about his Father and their Spirit. Jesus is the least among humans, even as God, and therefore the greatest, and not just in those years between his birth and his death but at every moment from the beginning of all things to their consummation.

The human God is not a celebrity and doesn't need or want to be famous. Jesus doesn't need his words, thoughts, or actions magnified on screens or through speakers, doesn't seek the adulation of the masses (Isa. 42:2). He does the quiet, unassuming, small things with great generosity, and needs nothing in return. That is how he lived and died, and that is how he brought all things into being and how he has cared for all things from the first.

A celebrity is by definition rarely a cross-bearer. It's to our incalculable poverty as a society to hold them up as models for how to live, to covet their spotlight, to desire their status. Whereas Isaiah says there was "nothing beautiful or majestic about [the Lord's] appearance, nothing to attract us to him. He was despised and rejected—a man of sorrows, acquainted with deepest grief. We turned our backs on him and looked the other way" (53:2–3 NLT).

Humility is God's way of life; therefore, it is the way to a life that is great as God is great. That said, we don't serve as a means of becoming "great"; we don't seek to be "last" only in order eventually to be exalted as "first." We are called by the love of God to love as God loves—by giving ourselves in anonymous labor for the good of all things. If we live to love others without recognition or privilege, we will participate by grace in the greatness God simply is.

I just took in a deep breath and so have been breathing all day. God never once shows up and asks me to thank him for those breaths, the air to breathe, the body to breathe it with. Today I ate food that God causes everywhere always to grow, and he did not show up at my meal demanding recognition. The sun rose this morning and will set this evening. The world and all other celestial bodies are held, yet again, in their wondrous trajectories, and God is not now demanding an ovation.

The human God works as the best servants do: imperceptibly. This seems odd to us because the world thinks of power as showy and imposing, but love abandons arrogance and adorns herself with poverty. Jesus shows us that there's room for all that God is in a simply human life.

Jesus shows us that there's room for all that God is in a simply human life.

The news that God is human in this way is a revolution. God shows up among us as a servant, a slave, because that is the human experience that most exemplifies the actual life that is God: "Jesus called them together and said, 'You know that the rulers in this world lord it over their people, and officials flaunt their authority over those under them. But among you it will be different. Whoever wants to be a leader among you must be your servant, and whoever wants to be first among you must become your slave. For even the Son of Man came not to be served but to serve others and to give his life as a ransom for many'" (Matt. 20:25–28 NLT).

The Son of God could become nothing else among us—a king, a general, an influencer—without distorting our understanding of God or without underwriting all our misunderstandings. God is not, as one pastor-theologian suggested, a God-centered God. This God does not exalt himself.

Jesus shows the path of co-suffering love—the cruciform road marked by suffering—to be the way to life and exaltation. How unlike fallen consciousness God is: craving recognition and power, disdaining anonymity, wanting control, desiring visibility, needing praise, acknowledgment, kudos.

Jesus tells us, "If you cling to your life, you will lose it; but if you give up your life for me, you will find it" (Matt. 10:39 NLT). Jesus is not talking merely about the exchange of our mortal existence for immortality. Jesus is describing how *everything* works. Yet this trust—that to give your life away is to keep your life—is not going to get you anywhere in what we have made of the world. If you live and act on this trust, you will be crucified.

You can serve the crucifying world that Christ loved before it loved him by embracing his sacred path of humility and by renouncing all other ways and means of power. You can serve power or you can serve humility—either and only one of these—but the world around you will experience the consequences of that choice.

If you are looking for God, look in every circumstance and in every place for the One who makes himself of no account, who takes a towel at every meal and kneels to serve you and the whole creation; for the One who does not stand outside your pain in denial or avoidance but who enters into every moment of your shame, despair, grief, and hurt and makes it his own; for the One who never abandons you, never stops hoping; for the One who keeps no record of wrongs, makes no boasts; for the One who is kind and patient; for the One who believes in you even when you no longer believe in yourself or even in him. Look, in other words, for Love.

We find this serving-all-things Love everywhere, in the most ordinary places, in the middle of the day or at the end of night. This Love arrives unexpectedly and often takes us by surprise.

PHOTINI

Jesus is tired and thirsty. He has been walking since daybreak in the sun's full strength. The One who made the sun and all the waters that reflect it now sweats in the heat he has made and is parched. The One who faints not, who never grows weary, needs a breather.

The fastest way home to Galilee from Jerusalem runs straight through a town in Samaria, right by the land and the well of his ancestor Jacob, who died almost twenty centuries before. Jesus, his feet sore, sits down on the ancient well. Wherever there's water in the universe, he is its source, and yet here he has no means to draw up a drink from the subterranean flow, some one hundred feet down and fed by a spring.

A woman approaches the well with a large pitcher on her shoulder, and when she arrives, Jesus asks her for a drink. There are layers of complication around this meeting, this moment, and this request for water (John 4:1–42).

Jewish men of Jesus's time and culture almost never speak to women in public (even their wives), and this woman is a Samaritan, of "impure" genetics and impure doctrine, a heretic. Sometimes for humans, no one is more "other" than the person who claims to worship the same God we worship but differently, and the Samaritans were "those people."

To make matters worse, the woman has come to the well alone. Jesus breaks all conventions, save the rule of love, when he initiates a conversation with her. But Love is getting ready to save the world, and Love knows what Love is doing.

Careful readers of Scripture recognize the shape of the story that is forming. We have been here before. A man and a woman meeting at a well signals the beginning of a marriage, a romance. Isaac, Jacob, and Moses—they all met their wives at a well like this one. Jesus has arrived at Sychar to initiate a courtship.

If we are paying attention, giving the Scriptures the attention that they train us to give all things, we know that what is unfolding at this roadside well is the keeping of a deep-seated promise that the God who is Love makes to the world and to all humanity. God desires to marry not just the woman but her people and not just the Samaritans but all nations, along with the lands and waters they inhabit. This God thirsts not only for water but also for union with us and with all creation.

This God thirsts not only for water but also for union with us and with all creation.

And God brings a wedding gift to the well.

The woman is surprised a Jewish man is asking a Samaritan woman for water, and Jesus shows his hand: "If you knew the gift of God and who it is that is saying to you, 'Give me a drink,' you would have asked him, and he would have given you living water" (John 4:10). It's the only time this particular Greek word for "gift" appears in the New Testament outside the book of Acts, and as in that history of the first Christians, here at the well the gift is the Spirit. None of us receive the Spirit apart from Jesus, the One who *gives* the gift, the One who *is* the gift.

"Living water" is moving water, like the waters of a spring, like the waters that feed this well. The woman wonders aloud how a man without a traveling skin with which to draw water from the well's depths somehow has water to give her. Jesus answers her, "Everyone who drinks of this water will be thirsty again, but those who drink of the water that I will give them will never be thirsty. The water that I will give will become in them a spring of water gushing up to eternal life" (John 4:13–14).

The woman asks Jesus for his never-failing water. She assumes he means the stuff in rivers and oceans, the stuff we are made of, the stuff we need every day to survive, but Jesus as ever wants to get to the heart of the matter. He asks the woman—the first Christians called her Photini, meaning "illumined one"—to go and get her husband.

But we learn from Jesus that Photini has had many husbands and that she now lives with a man in the absence of any promise. Perhaps this is why she is alone. Is she driven to avoid the company of the women of her city by their shaming, forced by their shunning to fetch her water unescorted in the midday heat?

In *Antiquities of the Jews* (AD 93–94), the historian Josephus recalls that when the Assyrians invaded the ten northern tribes of Israel, carrying many of the Jews of that region into a captive exile, the Assyrians brought in peoples from five other nations they had conquered (10.184). Each people group worshiped a different god and intermarried with the Jews who remained.

The Samaritans were the people who emerged from that invasion, that displacement, and that mingling, and while the Samaritans still observed Torah, they were unwelcome at the temple in Jerusalem, so they built their own temple in the fifth century BC (a temple that a Jewish ruler destroyed almost three centuries later).

This has led both ancient and contemporary readers of John's Gospel to speculate that when Jesus refers to the woman's husbands, he means the gods worshiped by the five Assyrian-conquered peoples, and to surmise that "the man she lives with now" is Caesar, for whom Herod had built a temple in the Samaritan capital dedicated to the worship of a living human emperor.

These interpreters recall that the rabbis allowed for two (and in rare cases three) marriages and assume that there's no reason to believe that the Samaritans were more permissive. Five legal husbands? Very unlikely, they say. Anyway—let's be clear—the ancient world wasn't a place where women made decisions for themselves, however much influence they might have had underneath the surface of things. Marriages ended for all sorts of reasons, but women were rarely if at all free to decide what was happening to them.

We need not assume that Photini's past is a shameful one. Ephrem the Syrian (306–73) instructs us to ponder this woman's many misfortunes, surviving the deaths of many companions and caregivers. Ephrem rebukes the tradition for slandering her, writing that she is "married" once more, but chastely, to avoid social pressures (*Hymns on Virginity* 22). Whatever the case—gods or husbands, personal tragedies or male-centered society—Photini was, as her people were, as we often are, adrift and lonely in the thirst for redemption, looking for love in all the wrong places.

When Jesus reveals that he knows her story better than she knows herself, she calls him a prophet. Prophets back then didn't make a lot of hay over sexual histories, but they cared a lot about who you worshiped.

Jesus, her prophet, perhaps looking up from the well to the ruins of the Samaritans' demolished temple on nearby Mount Gerizim, seeks her well-being: "Woman, believe me, the hour is coming when you will worship the Father neither on this mountain nor in Jerusalem. The hour is coming and is now here when the true worshipers will worship the Father in spirit and truth, for the Father seeks such as these to worship him. God is spirit, and those who worship him must worship in spirit and truth" (John 4:21, 23–24).

Photini, filled with the Spirit (and with anticipation) after Jesus tells her everything she has ever done, replies, "I know that Messiah is coming" (who is called Christ). "When he comes, he will proclaim all things to us." Jesus responds, "I am he, the one who is speaking to you" (John 4:25–26). Or as John Behr renders the Greek, "I AM, the one talking to you."[1]

Jesus invokes the divine name spoken to Moses from the burning-but-not-consumed bush, and eternity awakens in her heart. She drinks the water that never evaporates, the water that *remains*, that stays with and in us in all the dark and hard places, even in death, and that keeps us for and through eternity.

Like Hagar, Photini can say of God, "He saw me; and then I saw him!" (Gen. 16:13 Message). Photini has in Jesus met the angel who rescued Ishmael (and Hagar) with living water from a hidden well in the wilderness of Beersheba.

Photini, like Paul, sees and hears Christ and is converted. She becomes an apostle of Jesus Christ, for "with [Christ] is the fountain of life" (Ps. 36:9). She sees the glory of the unseen Father shining on the sweaty, sun-kissed face of the Son, and like her names suggests, her heart is illumined. Jesus becomes her seventh and final bridegroom.

She returns to her city, leaving her water pitcher behind as the disciples left their nets (for she now has the forever water flowing from her), and bears witness to everyone that Christ is now here.

Yes, it's a question she poses to her neighbors—"Can this be the Christ?"—but we sense that this suggestion is *rhetorical*, proclaimed from a sure and certain hope that if her neighbors by the Spirit drink the water given to her, they too will be changed.

At Photini's inspired invitation, the people of the city go out to the well with her to see the anointed One for themselves, and as they cross the open fields, walking toward Jesus and the disciples, Jesus points to the approaching crowds and says, "Look around you, and see how the fields are ripe for harvesting" (John 4:35).

Jesus finds a bride in Photini and in the whole Samaritan people, who see him as not only the Savior of the Jews and their Savior but also "the Savior of the world" (John 4:42; see also 1 John 4:14), a title attributed to the Caesars. They welcome him to stay with them. And he does.

The rabbis believed that a boundless reservoir existed under the old temple in Jerusalem and that in the last days this water would pour out from the temple's right side and fill the world.

The rabbis were remembering the words of Ezekiel 47:1–12, which the first Christians also took up in their antiphon at Easter, in the *Vidi Aquam*, where, as Ezekiel foresees, waters flow out from the temple and gradually flood the whole world, bringing verdant life and healing to everything they touch. Zechariah also prophesies about a "living water" that "will flow out from Jerusalem" (Zech. 14:8).

We hear Jesus say to Photini, and later to the gathered crowds in the temple in Jerusalem at Sukkot, that he has living water to give anyone who is thirsty, for any person who wants a drink. And we remember that the evangelist tells us in John 7 that this living water is the Spirit and that the *source* of this living water (this gift) is the new temple that is Christ's body.

When we stand with the women and with John at the cross, as Jesus exhales his last breath and releases his Spirit, and as the soldier lances the postmortem body of Jesus and water flows from his right side, we begin to see that here on Golgotha the Holy Spirit is being poured out on all flesh, and the living waters are filling all the world, from the right side of Christ's body, the true temple, and in the glorious words of the *Vidi Aquam*, "All those who drink are saved."[2]

Paul tells the Corinthians, "We were all made to drink of one Spirit" (1 Cor. 12:13), and *by this drinking*, the Spirit has made us all Photinis—temples of the bright presence of Christ in the midst of the world, his living water flowing out from us to bring his life everywhere and to everyone.

EVERYONE

I walked around a good part of the southern end of New York's Central Park on a spring day not long ago. The diversity of humans is exhilarating. You can discern, if you slow down and pay attention, something of how very different everyone is from everyone else. Manhattan is such an inhabited island; more than 1.6 million people reside on it.

That day, walking in and around some of those humans, overhearing bits of conversation, watching anger or worry or wonder or confusion flash across this stranger's face or that one, I found myself pondering what sort of lives they live and what sort of loves inspire their existence. Why are they here? What do they want? What do they fear? What makes them cry? What makes them sing? How do they pray? What do they know of God that I have yet to learn?

Feeling something of my difference from them and their difference from each other brought home to me how hard it can be to know and be known. It made me ask, perhaps for the first time, how one human being could possibly relate in an undeniable and intimate way with all of them. Is Jesus that human? It seems we ought to allow the question and sit with it.

There are so many cultures, languages, paradigms, influences, histories, injuries, thoughts, desires, traumas, loves, and so much else rooted, jumbled up, and often opposed within us. What sort of person could bring all that together? Who can put all of humanity in the same room and at the same table? So that no one is left out?

Somewhere in his kaleidoscopic heart is not only the wisdom that makes this enormous and beautiful diversity we call humanity but also the divine fire that ignites the energy we experience in each human we encounter.

The thing about Jesus is that as the Son of God he is the Maker of us all. So somewhere in his kaleidoscopic heart is not only the wisdom that makes this enormous and beautiful diversity we call humanity but also the divine fire that ignites the energy we experience in each human we encounter.

Jesus is also the God who becomes what he makes, who becomes human. He lived his own life, we might say, but his life was not merely his own. Jesus took upon himself *all* that it means to be human in all the myriad ways every human is human in all the moments and places of this world. And Jesus gives life to the humanity we, each of us, are together, the embodied reality every living soul shares with every living soul.

From eternity, but also at just the right moment in the human story, when God chose to unveil God within the world we see, touch, taste, smell, and hear, when God chose to take on visible and vulnerable materiality, the one God Genesis describes with a communal word—"us"—chose of all things in creation to become human. Gregory of Nyssa, a fourth-century pastor, elevates our humanity:

> Know to what extent the Creator has honored you above all the rest of Creation: the sky is not an image of God, nor is the moon,

> nor the sun, nor the beauty of the stars, nor anything of what can be seen in Creation. You alone have been made the image of the Reality that transcends all understanding, the likeness of Imperishable Beauty, the imprint of True Divinity, the recipient of Beatitude, the seal of the True Light. When you turn to him you become that which he is himself. Nothing in Creation can be compared with your greatness. God is able to measure the whole heaven with his span. The earth and the sea are enclosed in the hollow of his hand. And although he is so great and holds all Creation in the palm of his hand, you are able to hold him. He dwells in you and moves within you without constraint, for he has said, "I will live and move among them."[1]

God becomes human and nothing else. In the estimation of God, nothing else in creation was as suitable for the dwelling of divinity as a human person. Herbert McCabe says that the command against making images of God was given because when we make idols, we end up ignoring the image of God in the one place it exists in creation: in every human.[2]

Remember: God does not become what is not good, and God does not become what God does not love. God does not give up on what God becomes. Humans are in the beginning made very good, and this created goodness remains in humanity despite all disfigurement.

It is true that our present humanity is broken and a mess, and (so far as I can tell) we are more capable than any visible thing in creation of the worst evils imaginable. Yet God considers us worthy of the divine image and likeness, worthy of being united forever to the divine life, worthy of measureless love. We are a mess, but we are God's mess.

No matter the distance our hearts and minds sail from God, God is in Jesus Christ our stowaway. I trust that he is the human who can have and does have and will have an undeniable and personal connection with all of us—including everyone I saw that day in Central Park. Because of his relation to us and to God, Jesus Christ is inside the experience of what it is to be every sort of human there is.

Dietrich Bonhoeffer says even more about the people who every day pass by you and me: "[Jesus] comes in the form of the beggar, of the dissolute human child in ragged clothes, asking for help. He confronts you in every person that you meet. As long as there are people, Christ will walk the earth as your neighbor, as the one through whom God calls you, makes demands on you."[3]

This ought to be scandalous to us, that God confronts us in everyone we encounter, that God is vulnerable like *that*. But this is what we trust when we trust that God has united himself to everyone in the humanity of Jesus.

God is not compressed or downsized into the authentic human reality of Jesus, not made something less than the Creator of all worlds and the fountain of all wisdom when taking on flesh. And the contingent, fragile, and limited humanity of Christ is not made invulnerable in one cell, in one sacred molecule, by union with divinity. Jesus is genuinely, perilously human.

The kindler of fire in a hundred trillion stars grows cold unless drawn to Mary's warm breast. The boy holding Joseph's lathe is the One whose power causes every tree in every forest of the world to grow in splendor and majesty.

The One who labors for each gasp of air in the fatal posture of crucifixion gives the breath of life to mountain goats and dolphins and starlings and every respirating creature resting on a thousand plains, swimming in a thousand streams.

This human Jesus, come among us, is the measure of God. In a hymn Paul borrows from the first Christians, he describes the Son's descent to human flesh: "Though he was God, he did not think of equality with God as something to cling to. Instead, he gave up his divine privileges [not his divinity!]; he took the humble position of a slave and was born as a human being. When he appeared in human form, he humbled himself in obedience to God and died a criminal's death on a cross" (Phil. 2:6–8 NLT).

It was not self-abasement for the Son of God to appear in our skin or to be numbered as one of us humans or to be among us as a servant. God loves being human. God is the servant among us. The humiliation was in the shameful manner of his death. Even so, the cross is where the Son of God shows us what it means to be human by dying in the way that he dies.[4] One early Christian says it like this: "The human being is earth that suffers."[5]

In a moment leading up to the cross, Pilate unintentionally acts as both prophet and apostle when he shouts, "Ecce homo"—behold the man (John 19:5). Behold *the human* among humans, the human who suffers as and with and for everyone.

This is the *mind* that is in the heart of Jesus Christ: not to love his life but to die for those his Father loves. The Greek word for this kind of devotion is *kenōsis*. God knows we like to argue about who is the greatest, but he is among us as a slave, as humility itself, as earth that suffers.

"Do you love me?" When Jesus asks Peter this question (John 21:15), he is asking it of us as well. He asks it and keeps asking until we realize that he is asking if we love *everyone* as he loves them, for he makes no distinction between himself and all humans—past, present, and future. The same love he has for his mother, the same love he has for his Father is the love he has for each one of us, always, and the love he gives us to love others.

When the Word became flesh and moved into our cities and villages, it was the eyes of the would-be executed woman who beheld him, and the shifty hands of the tax collector who in invitation took his hand. It was the heart of the doubter, ravaged by existential questions, and the hate-tortured hearts of persecutors—grown-up temple-attending and law-abiding bullies—that first heard the voice of humanity's Good Shepherd.

And what they saw and heard was the Love that created them and the Love that desired them above all else, a fire of Love that would burn in them, purging every deficit of love and making them lanterns that shine with the uncreated light of a kingdom that will never end. In the end, and by his patience, we pray, all of us will shine like the sun.

SHEPHERD

The words of the song are so familiar that we can forget there was a time in the world when Psalm 23 did not exist.

The song came from a man who as a boy herded sheep for his father. In the imagination that shaped and fired the memory of Israel, David was not a warrior first nor a king but a poet, a minstrel. This song and other songs emerged from his experience as a working shepherd-poet.

To our minds, David is mythic, larger than life. Yet his was not an idyllic world but the same world as ours: a world of storms and fires, predators and prey, famines and hoarded resources, stretches and bursts of violence as well as moments of stolen tranquility. From his youth, David fed, shielded, rescued, and cared for his sheep, and he came to feel in his bones how the God of his ancestors was all the things to him he had to be to his flock.

Israel's poets were not the first in the ancient world to speak of the gods as shepherds. But against the tendency to speak of the gods as apathetic or cruel, indifferent and punishing, capricious and inconstant, David celebrates his God as a *good* shepherd. His God isn't a presence faraway and aloof but a friend close and personal. Alone in the wilderness, David came to feel what Moses before him had known: God's nearness and tender attention.

David's psalm identifies God as a shepherd like himself, who leads humanity through the fragile wilderness of this world to a goodness and permanence unknown to us by a journey through death to life.

This Good Shepherd was not a god David conjured or fancied to meet his expectations and personal needs but the Creator—the presence in his life of guidance, provision, protection, and love. At some point, who knows when, a song arose in him—and so we have it now, all these years later, and we can pray it and sing it not only after him but also with him.

Jesus prayed and sang Psalm 23 with his Scripture-saturated mother and others in his home synagogue. He took the song to heart and made it his own.

At some point, who knows when, perhaps as the words of the song were still sweet on his lips, words authored in the heart of David, words made for the mouth of the Messiah, Jesus recognized himself: "I am the good shepherd." These words must have exploded in him, filled his heart as only a song can fill a heart in that moment.

The Lord of Psalm 23 has taken on flesh. Jesus is the shepherd who enters the sheepfold by the door, whose voice the sheep recognize, whose rod and staff the wolf and the bear fear, who leads and guides and protects us.

Jesus says there is a robber, a hireling, who comes to steal, kill, and destroy, who abandons the sheep, who does not care for them, while Jesus guards the sheep by laying down his life for them. And all the sheep of all the pastures of the world come together around the altar where Jesus offers his life, and at the end of the world there is only one flock under one shepherd, singing one song.

Ancient Christians depicted Jesus in paintings as a shepherd with sheep at his feet, a young ewe resting on his shoulders, and sometimes a protecting and rescuing staff in his hand—the One they knew as the Good Shepherd. They experienced in Jesus the words of Isaiah: "He will feed his flock like a shepherd; he will gather the lambs in his arms and carry them in his bosom and gently lead the mother sheep" (Isa. 40:11). John of Damascus speaks for them: "You have humbled yourself, Christ my God, so that you might carry me, your stray sheep, on your shoulders."[1]

The mothers and fathers of the church, as well as her seers and singers, spoke often of this Good Shepherd. But can humans know the Good? Not everyone thinks so. They say humans are too wicked, too broken—are "totally depraved"—and so cannot trust their instincts and intuitions about what constitutes good and evil, much less grasp the Good that is beyond all we know or understand.

Yet the best of the Christian tradition understands that our intuitions about evil come from our share in the image of God. It is that image that makes us desire good and the Good. Athanasius says that God fashioned human beings to perceive and understand reality through their likeness to God (*Contra Gentes* 2.2).

It is the image of God in the human, the soil and seed of goodness the Gardener has nurtured in us, that recoils when we hear certain teachers claim that God does evil or that we are never able to know whether what God is said to have done is or is not good. We are troubled, and rightly so, when people talk as if God kills, steals, and destroys. It is a demonic doctrine that evil can be called good and good, evil. What satan wants is for us not to know good and evil but to confuse them as he has confused them.

The human God is in every moment of his life among us the antithesis of this whispered confusion, this veiled accusation, showing us always and everywhere what God is like and that God is good and only good. Where we or the dark powers have made a muddle of the image of God, Jesus is here to show us who God is and who we are.

The Good Shepherd of the sheep is like other good shepherds—only more so. His goodness is so good we might at times, driven by the fear of death and tormented by the evil one, fail to recognize it. But he is always better than good, never less.

Jesus, we confess, is God in exactly the same sense the Father and the Spirit are God. Therefore, God is like Christ, and as Michael Ramsey says, "God is Christlike, and in him is no un-Christlikeness at all."[2] If we cannot imagine the divine and human person we encounter in the Scriptures doing or saying something that brings harm, even unintentionally, to anyone or anything, then we cannot and should not imagine God doing that harm, for Jesus is God made visible. Jesus is the Word God has to speak, the truth and the beauty and the goodness of all things.

If we cannot imagine the divine and human person we encounter in the Scriptures doing or saying something that brings harm, even unintentionally, to anyone or anything, then we cannot and should not imagine God doing that harm.

The image in which humans were made is broken and corrupted in us—no doubt about it. We can be petty and ignorant, stupid and cruel, devious and judgmental. We sometimes see wickedness where it is not, and we leave so much good undone because we fail to see the need for and possibility of it.

It is far more often the case that in our confusion about who we are, in our fear and need for control, we name something good that is evil, something like torture, and try to excuse ourselves and our involvement in it by denying its wickedness, or by underwriting it in the name of God. Still, it is obvious to others, and at times apparent to us as well, that we are trying to convince ourselves of a lie our hearts know better than to believe.

David Bentley Hart has helped me many times to regain the awareness that God is a Good Shepherd. He writes, "If it is from Christ that we are to learn how God relates himself to sin, suffering, evil, and death, it would seem that he provides us little evidence of anything other than a regal, relentless, and miraculous enmity: sin he forgives, suffering he heals, evil he casts out, and death he conquers. And absolutely nowhere does Christ act as if any of these things are part of the eternal work or purposes of God."[3]

Some readers of Job use him to make the Lord more like Janus then Jesus, but they are not reading Job well. Yes, Job says, "The LORD gave, and the LORD has taken away; blessed be the name of the LORD" (Job 1:21), and we shouldn't ignore Job's sense of things as a husband and father in deep pain. But because we know the character of our God, the God of Israel, we know this cannot mean, as some teach, that all things—all goods and all evils—come from God.

God gives the good, always and only the good: "Every generous act of giving, with every perfect gift, is from above, coming down from the Father of lights, with whom there is no variation or shadow due to change" (James 1:17).

God takes away only what is not for our good and takes away only for our good. God will kill in us all that is not of love but will not do any harm to us in that killing. God will steal evil from the world but will leave all created goods, including humans, better than they are in the taking away of what can be shaken. God's fiery desire for our good will destroy all in us and in the creation that is disordered and chaotic but grants all things abundant life and permanence in their dismantling.

Job's words are seen in their true light when they are transfigured for us by the person of Jesus. Jesus is not the one who brings death, theft, or destruction (John 10:10). He is the One who saves us from evil, who transfigures evil as only God can (Gen. 50:20), not the one who intends or uses it.

In the humanity of Jesus, we see that divine sovereignty has a different character than we would have expected. It has little or nothing to do with what we think it means to "be in control." Paul's words are clear: Love does no wrong. It also rejoices not in the wrong but only in the right, the good (1 Cor. 13:6).

By essence, love is never coercive, never violent as we are violent. The divine love wounds at times but, as with a good surgeon, only to heal. Rather than doing wrong, love bears all wrongs and bears them without wronging even the wrongdoers.

Jesus is tortured and violated, and yet he never retaliates or loses faith in the Father whose goodness cannot be overcome or undone: "When he was abused, he did not return abuse; when he suffered, he did not threaten, but he entrusted himself to the one who judges justly. He himself bore our sins in his body on the cross, so that, having died to sins, we might live for righteousness; by his wounds you have been healed. For you were going astray like sheep, but now you have returned to the shepherd and guardian of your souls" (1 Pet. 2:23–25).

Seeing Christ on his cross, we know that God is able and more than able to carry and to cure all things, and we remember that there is no greater participation in healing than to remain with someone in their dying. We know Jesus can and will answer every prayer for rescue by joining us in every suffering—every last one. In the end that God is bringing, he will end all evils because divine weakness is stronger than every pretension to power.

The nails driven into the flesh of Christ make vain all human, demonic, and anti-Christian imagination that the God who creates and upholds the world by love is in some other "part" of himself the one who destroys the world.

The nails driven into the flesh of Christ are also the nails driven into the coffin of the idea that the living God sends evil or participates in crimes or desires the death of anyone. There is a destroyer, but his false, murderous way of violence, abuse, coercion, and death is defeated by the humility of God.

In the meantime, when we encounter evil, we trust, we know that God is not behind it. Instead, he is with us in it and against it, overturning it from without and from within. The Good Shepherd can and does convert the evil we experience to our good, converts for our good what is intended for evil as only God can. He does so by laying down his life for the sheep and by suffering like a sheep.

> He was oppressed, and he was afflicted,
> yet he did not open his mouth;
> like a lamb that is led to the slaughter,
> and like a sheep that before its shearers is silent,
> so he did not open his mouth. (Isa. 53:7)

When I preach or write about the love of our Father in this way, there's always someone who says, "Don't forget to preach the other side of the story."

What other side? That God has something bad or imperfect in store for us, perhaps a snake or a stone instead of bread and fish? That God gives only to take back the gift? That God cannot be trusted?

God does not have "sides." Everything in God is in union. Our God is not—like the lesser gods, like many human fathers—many-sided, contradictory, or inconsistent. There is no shifting shadow in God (James 1:17). We may not always understand his goodness, but he is always and only good.

God *is* love. Love is not an attribute or part or side or angle of God. Love is the *name* of God (1 John 4:9–10).

Yet when it comes to evil, we are bewildered by the apparent inattention of God. Why doesn't God always intervene to stop it? We should be unafraid to sit with this question as long as we or anyone else needs to sit with it. And as we sit, perhaps it's instructive to ponder divine patience, coupled with what God *has* done about evil in Jesus Christ.

The world that *is* is the world we humans have made through countless decisions and acts offered up in pursuit of an ever-elusive "happiness." We have sought to bend all things to our will; the cumulative effect of those efforts over thousands of years is staggering.

The collective weight of human sin is sobering. Most of the time we don't allow ourselves to reflect on this because it's too hard to bear. The world God creates is subject to our human choices, and after each and every choice it is simply, unalterably the world we choose and no other.

Under the sway of sin, humans choose an existence other than the one God intends for us. And that choosing brings with it dire consequences. We can ask why God does not keep us from our sins or save us from their consequences, but the answer is already obvious. For the good of the world and in his wisdom, God restrains himself when he *could* intervene to prevent or thwart our brute evil, our carelessness, our callous and cavalier treatment of others, our self-destructive impulses, even our clumsiness and ignorance. He shows restraint because he is not evil and is never moved by fear. Love bears all things, and we force that burden on him by all that we do that is not done in love. Humans cannot undo any action or word of ours that opposes the love that God is, and so the world and all things and persons in it experience disintegration, chaos, and death.

What if there is a human whose choices and words remake the broken world into the world God intended from before time and whose life mends all the chaos and death? Not by erasing or reversing or undoing history but by redeeming and healing every human choice.

God is good beyond our wildest hopes. We know this because a particular human teaches us to forgive and not condemn, to heal and not curse, to free and not chain, to die and not kill. This sacred opposition to all that harms his image bearers was revealed in stone on Sinai as the very being of God but never understood until the life of God in human flesh ended without ever taking one life.

The marks of his wounds remain on this vulnerable One who redeems the world, and the cruel cross on which we attempted to snuff out his light and life is not in the end seen as though it never occurred. No, that is not how the living God heals us or his world. This God works with the fractured reality we have made. He works with our nails and our rust and our crown of thorns.

The unthinkable evil that occurs on Golgotha is transfigured by the Father, who raises from futility and destruction the only endlessly faithful human who has ever existed and—this is so wondrous—makes his Son's holy life and self-sacrificial love the center and measure of every human's life. He does this because that is the kind of God he is and the kind of love he shares with the Son and the Spirit from eternity.

An ancient midrash tells us that a baby goat wandered away from Moses and his flock. Moses searches and finds the goat drinking from a stream and gently says, "I did not know that you ran away because of thirst."[4] For this mercy, God entrusts to Moses the future of Israel and the hope of the world.

Chabad Rabbi Menachem Schneerson, commenting on this midrash, writes, "Moses realized that the kid did not run away from the flock out of malice or wickedness—it was merely thirsty. . . . Only a shepherd who hastens not to judge the runaway kid, who is sensitive to the causes of its desertion, can mercifully lift it into his arms and bring it back home."[5] How often we misunderstand people when they leave our fold! It would help, I think, to be sensitive to the causes rather than to assign blame or shame. God never misunderstands.

The beautiful Shepherd puts us before himself, values the life of his flock over his own life. This means that every human is loved by God more than God loves his own life. We do not say this enough, or plainly. And this is one of many reasons the churches are emptying. Knowing all our hidden thoughts and everything we do that no one sees, he *still* values our lives over his.

John the beloved tells us that we likewise should lay down our lives by giving of ourselves and our property to our brother in need (1 John 3:16). God never asks us to do anything that he does not enable in us by his Spirit. Every invitation to participate in the goodness of our Good Shepherd carries the blessing to do so.

We are, after all, not saved by what we do or don't do or by what we believe or don't believe. We are saved by God because it is simply the nature of God to save what God loves.

We can trust ourselves and others with this human God. Jesus is a more beautiful and good Shepherd than we have been told. He waits every morning and night of the world for our words and glances, sighs and groans. He rejects nothing we bring to him, even the hardest, inexpressible things. His love handles and heals it all. All through the long night of our existence, he lies as the gate for his flock, his body between us and the wolves. And when we are afraid, he sings over us.

HEALER

Theologian Ben Myers says that Jesus is the human "who marches through all the stages of our life without ever once taking his eyes off of [the Father], and in that way he lives out a fully human life that is always responding to God in love."[1] In living this way, Jesus overwrites the broken way of living a human life that entered the world with Adam and Eve, heals the living of a human life down to its core. He lives a complete human life for us as God so that his life is now your life and my life and every human life.

So, we can say that becoming human is a journey: Jesus continues to become flesh in every moment of the Gospels. Everything he says and does and everything he is for humanity during his life among us is Christ becoming flesh of our flesh and bone of our bone—temptations, persecutions, betrayals, grief, pain, hunger, poverty, death—and it does not stop there. Jesus carries the incarnation into eternity, reconciling the human nature we all share to God. As Dorothy Sayers puts it with her usual punch:

> For whatever reason God chose to make man as he is—limited and suffering and subject to sorrows and death—he [God] has the honesty and the courage to take his own medicine. Whatever game he is playing with this creation, he has kept his own rules and played fair. He can exact nothing from man that he has not

> exacted from himself. He has himself gone through the whole of human experience, from the trivial irritations of family life and the cramping restrictions of hard work and lack of money to the worst horrors of pain and humiliation, defeat, despair, and death. When he was a man, he played the man.[2]

Incarnation held in this way is an endless wonder. It is not just a conception and birth but an entire human life lived in its entirety in a new way—from infancy and childhood through adolescence into adulthood to death. And thanks to the Spirit who raised Christ from the dead, we can authentically live this new way of being human because the Father desires this for us. Christ's life can be our actual way of life in the world.

Karl Rahner says this can be true despite all our doubts. We can be kind and gentle and forgiving and hopeful and cheerful and serene and unsuspicious and loyal—can be human as God is human: "God himself has tried this [living a human life] and has told us that it works. His experience is more decisive and credible than ours: we can be better than we think."[3]

When God took on flesh, Christ took upon himself all ethnicities and cultures, in all times and places. There is no ethos, no mindset, no common life—in all the varieties of ways women and men have been human from primitive times until today—that is alien to Jesus. None. Jesus takes on the *one human nature* that every human shares, but the one human nature every human shares is embodied and spoken and lived out in a one-of-a-kind way by every human there is.

We can say it in this way and keep the train of sentences going for a long time: The Word became Chinese. The Word became a child of Allah. The Word became medieval. The Word became a street magician. The Word became a scientist.

The Word became a beggar. The Word became a thief. The Word became an artist. The Word became a Zulu and a Sioux. The Word became the pregnant mother. The Word became the expectant father. And so on.

But let's be clear: Christ's universality is not generic. It is total and founded on a definitive set of particulars. Jesus was a male descendant of David and Abraham; a Jew born under Roman occupation to a yielded-to-God teenager; a refugee immigrant in Egypt, where his forefather, Jacob's son Joseph, sojourned; a carpenter who set joists and planed boards. And so on. And precisely as the One who lived that life, he is the firstborn of all creation, the One in whom life was made, the life that is the light that enlightens everyone who comes into the world.

The universals are true because the particulars of his sacred life among us are genuine and saving and healing. All of them. Jesus's every thought and action, including those lost to history and those overlooked or ignored by his contemporaries, heal the human nature he shares with all humans.

I am saying it this way, coming at it from different angles—applying Jesus to everyone, everywhere, always—finally to say what Gregory Nazianzen, an ancient Christian pastor, said: "That which is not assumed is not healed. That which is united to God, *that* will be saved. If half of Adam fell, also half will be taken up and saved. But if all of Adam fell, all of his nature will be united to God, and all of it will be saved."[4] Gregory is echoing Paul: "For as all die in Adam, so all will be made alive in Christ" (1 Cor. 15:22).

Jesus is a walking, talking Tree of Life. His incarnation heals everything. Even touching the fringe of Jesus's robe brings restoration. The lame walk. The blind see. Leprosy vanishes. Limbs grow back. The dead are raised. Jürgen Moltmann says more: "When Jesus expels demons and heals the sick, he is driving out of creation the powers of destruction, and is healing and restoring created beings who are hurt and sick. . . . Jesus' healings are not supernatural miracles in a natural world. They are the only truly 'natural' thing in a world that is unnatural, demonized and wounded."[5]

In being humanity's healer, Jesus wants to draw no attention to himself, wants to remain hidden.

In being humanity's healer, Jesus wants to draw no attention to himself, wants to remain hidden. Jesus wants only to be available to our wounds, as Athanasius explains: "The Lord came not to be put on display but to heal and to teach those who were suffering. One being put on display only needs to appear and dazzle the beholders."[6] Jesus needs to do no such tricks; virtue simply radiates out from him to heal anyone in any crowd, and only Jesus and the person he touches notice.

For more than twenty years, I have served a parish in one of the "safest" suburbs in America and served its county as a first responder. I can testify to the fact that evil doesn't discriminate. There is as much spiritual mayhem here as anywhere, as much bewildering evil now as in the ancient world. The world is not well, we are not well, and sobriety asks us to show up and admit it. The healing that the human God brings is needed everywhere.

One of the reasons the Gospels have the kind of power they do for so many is that they do not shrink from reality. They tell it like it is. They are not in denial about the corners into which we humans have painted ourselves.

Luke's story of a man living a tortured existence in a cemetery by a rural lakeshore—he, his family, and his community afflicted in different degrees by spiritual darkness—makes as much sense in Luke's time as it does in ours (8:26–39).

The demons Jesus confronts don't want to be sent back to "the abyss," whatever that is. One wonders what the abyss must be like because they'd rather inhabit a herd of pigs than go back there. You see, the pigs, for all their piggish existence, are yet part of the creation God made good.

It was Stephen Hawking who described the boundary of a black hole, the "event horizon," as a place where one might hang a sign with the words of Dante: "Abandon all hope ye who enter here."[7] But it seems the abyss is something rather worse.

The Oxford High School shooting, after which I informed and held the families who lost their children, felt like entering the abyss. Most humans in our war-torn, poverty-stricken, and disease-addled world live many frightening moments suffering evil. Some of the evil confronts us in smaller moments.

Once when I was on the phone with a young woman suffering from an eating disorder who had been committed for last-resort care, it felt like a deep chill invaded the room, a resistance to the light I was trying to give voice to. I'll admit it frightened me, but I kept speaking words of life. Eventually, whatever felt it owned this young woman dissipated, and in the weeks and months to come, by the Spirit she eventually found liberty and wholeness.

When Jesus commanded the demons to depart from his desperate human brother, I imagine he spoke the command in a "still small voice," the one Elijah heard in the cave on Sinai, the whisper that wasn't in the wind, earthquake, or fire (1 Kings 19:12 RSV)—quiet, authentic words of a love that does not boast and yet can never be resisted or overcome by evil.

And after the stampede and the cliff and the drownings and the anger of the pig herders and the townsfolk's curiosity and the running to see what trouble Jesus had made for them, there was simply a fellow human made well—sitting at the feet of his rabbi, "clothed and in his right mind" (Luke 8:35). And for just one fleeting and brilliant moment, everyone was silenced by the holiness of it all. One day that moment will never end.

"Clothed and in his right mind." I know when I read those words that this story is true and that it's the truest story one can tell, not just of this man's life but of the life of anyone and everyone. Come what may, nothing is going to stop Love from clothing us all in himself and renewing in us all the mind of Christ, the One who sets all things right.

In the temple, Isaiah the prophet-priest sees, hears, and feels the presence of the Lord his God (Isa. 6:1–8).

His vision—the billowing robe, the wingèd ministers of fire who dart to and fro, the smoke, the throne—offers him a profound sense of his *difference* from all he sees, hears, and feels. And this recognition of difference is good for him and for us, so far as it goes, but it is neither the desire of God nor his purpose for Isaiah or for us to be condemned as we live in this awareness of difference.

God has no interest in reinforcing our frailty or shame. We may become aware of all these differences, this lack and unworthiness, when God reveals himself. We may in that moment feel exposed. But God doesn't desire to be our superior and so has no interest in making us feel inferior. God wants us to experience eternity in the ordinariness of the world, to experience our actual, inescapable union with and suitedness for his life and love.

Between Isaiah's vision and the divine request for someone to "go for us," the healing activity of God makes Isaiah aware there's something about himself, about all of us, that is truer than his sinfulness. Far beyond any difference, humans share a bedrock union with God.

The truest thing about us humans is that we are born in the loving conversation of God, that we come from the One who said, "Let *us* make humans in our image" (Gen. 1:26, emphasis added). We are the divine image in clay, the creature gifted to speak the creative word over the world, the word of promise about what God is bringing to her: the end of conflict, scarcity, sickness, predation, and death.

In Isaiah's vision of the Lord, a seraph takes a jewel of amber fire from the golden altar that stands near the veil that is, as we know from the book of Hebrews, Christ's flesh. He takes the burning coal that is full of light and heat but that somehow does no harm and places it to Isaiah's lips. And the fire that is God doesn't destroy Isaiah—it purifies him. This fire heals; it burns away sin. The fire enables him to speak of a transfigured world where the child from Bethlehem leads creation and all creatures to the peaceable kingdom. "With its fire, love makes better whatever it has touched,"[8] Ambrose, the fourth-century Milanese pastor, teaches.

When that fire touches our lips, we are healed, made ready to speak God's transfiguring words over the earth, made ready to join God's adventurous work to redeem the cosmos. This fire of Love makes Isaiah (and us) forever after a part of the divine conversation about the world that God is making of this world (despite all present appearances)—a world where we live as long as trees, without calamity and predators, a world that has become everywhere a holy mountain on which no one harms or destroys.

When receiving the bread and wine at Communion, when the same fiery love Isaiah receives is pressed to our lips, our response is to know ourselves as children of God and with Isaiah to reply, "Send us." Common bread on all the tables where it is offered as thanksgiving becomes suffused with the fire that is the life of the triune God. Two things—bread and Christ—become somehow one thing without ceasing to be what they are apart from each other.

We do not grasp for equality with God. But with and in Isaiah, and with and in Christ, we receive the crucible of humility and are found alive on the other side of the death we remember in this sacred meal, which will in time, Jesus promises, make us forever alive.

We take the Eucharist because we hope to become human. We eat Christ's body and drink Christ's blood because we desire to be healed and to be found in the likeness of God. It is the human God who is making of us his very self in the meal. Remember, the shepherds' sign in Bethlehem is a feed trough. Christ has come down so we can become what we eat: the body of Christ.

At this meal, every time we partake in it, we approach the transfiguring Light trusting in his deep goodness, trusting that the uncreated light of God that shines from the human face of Jesus Christ will burn away all that is not from God. It is only the works of God in us that survive when we leave the shadows of shame and gaze upon his furious, fiery love.

The death we remember at the Eucharist is the death of the human God. It is to a deep contemplation of that death (a death that is our dying also) that we now bravely turn, trusting that this death is also our life.

A HUMAN DEATH

We all indeed wish to be God with God, but God knows there are few of us who want to live as men with his humanity, or want to carry his cross with him, or want to hang on the cross.

—Hadewijch of Antwerp, Letter 6.227

Through the Passion, the one Lord Jesus Christ becomes, as human, that which he, as God, always is.

—John Behr, *John the Theologian and His Paschal Gospel*

The story of Jesus—which in its fullest extent is the entire Bible—is the projection of the trinitarian life of God on the rubbish dump that we have made of the world.

—Herbert McCabe, *God Matters*

MOUNTAIN

Peter knows he's as good as dead. Christians all over Rome are being killed because Nero blames the new religion for the fires that leveled two-thirds of the city, fires that ancient historians tell us the emperor himself set.

Peter will be one of thousands. More than three thousand others will perish with him—little ones, men and women, Jews and Romans, young and old, the enslaved and the "free." All because a powerful man told a powerful lie. As he faces his end, Peter realizes that he wants to be sure that those who remain remember something he once saw with his own eyes, something more real and true than anything else he witnessed in his life, something Nero's lie could not destroy.

He wants us to remember too, for the world is always on fire with lies.

Perhaps to our surprise, it is not the crucifixion that Peter has in mind, though the story he tells about the mountain is about the cross, as all good stories are. But Peter was not an eyewitness at Golgotha. He did not hear the torture, did not see the anguish. He fled.

No, Peter wants them to remember what happened just before all of that went down, when he and James and John ascended

Mount Tabor with Jesus. Transfiguration is what Peter most wants his readers, wants us, to remember.

As Peter's violent death looms, *this event on the mountain* is what he wants to set in the center of their hearts and our hearts. But why? Let's examine what he says about what happened in his preaching as recalled in the Gospels and in his second letter.

What Peter sees on that mountain happens just like he says it did. It happens in the world where babies are nursed and elders speak a final blessing over their heirs, where boats are at the mercy of the sea, where fish are caught and where sheep are fed, where an oil lamp is lit to fill a dark room with light. And it happens in a world where everything that is alive with beauty and goodness eventually withers and dies.

Peter says they saw the face of Jesus shining like the sun, his garments radiant with light incomparable, uncreated; he says they heard a conversation between the law in the person of Moses, the prophets in the person of Elijah, and their embodiment in Mary's son, Jesus. It was a conversation about his *exodus* to be accomplished in Jerusalem in God's blood (and Mary's).

Peter wants his flock to remember this moment—his eyewitness account of what happened on the holy mountain—for it will "be a light to you in dark places, when all other lights go out." Actually, that's a line from *The Lord of the Rings* when Galadriel gives Frodo the crystal bottle in which is "caught the light of Eärendil's star."[1] It sounds a lot like what Simon Peter says, for surely this saying of Peter's rang in J. R. R. Tolkien's heart. Simon Peter says, "You will do well to be attentive to this [moment on the mountain] as to a lamp shining in a dark place, until the day dawns and the morning star rises in your hearts" (2 Pet. 1:19).

Christians want to commemorate the transfiguration at least once a year in our worship because it is a revelation of the defeat of death. An elementary observation about the event demonstrates this and is often overlooked or unspoken.

On the mountain, Moses and Elijah, dead to history, are very much alive and, once again somehow in ways we do not fully understand, embodied. They are speaking with Jesus in audible voices. This is not telepathy. Human speech requires tongues and tongues require bodies. Heaven has opened and *they are there*, reflecting, perhaps, on what their sufferings mean in light of his as they talk about the Passover that this One—the human God—will accomplish in Jerusalem.

As they converse, Moses surely understands that the blood on the doorposts of Israel—the dark stains that warded off the "angel" of death long ago in Egypt—is mystically but truly the blood of this human with whom he and Elijah are speaking. What else could it be? It is in the end not the blood of sheep and goats that defeats death but the blood of God.

In the confident, vulnerable voice of Jesus, Elijah recognizes his Lord, the One who did not pass him by, who was not in the great and strong wind, or in the earthquake, or in the fire but in the still small voice.

Seeing and hearing Moses on the mountain, we remember that the law tastes good like honey, that if humanity could be converted by it—and we cannot—the earth would be a paradise free of murder, envy, lies, and disrespect.

Seeing and hearing Elijah, we recall that if Israel (or we) had listened to the prophets, the refugee would be welcome, the poor never neglected, the oppressed set free from enslavement, all debts canceled, but, God have mercy, we are blind and deaf.

By the transfiguration, we see that the law and the prophets are not ended; rather, in the radiant, inscripturated body of the Son—in the Word made flesh, the One who animates all scriptural wisdom—Israel's patriarchs, sages, and prophets find their *telos*, their perfection.

Peter, James, and John are witnessing a reach-out-and-touch-it experience of the resurrection, of something more real than our death-drunk reality.

Resurrection is just outside our ken, just beyond our ability to perceive it, and yet here on the mountain we see that it is nevertheless everywhere, and near us, and greater than death. Transfiguration shows us that resurrection, not death, is the end of all things.

Here on the holy mountain, for a fleeting moment of eternal now, the disciples also witness the glory of what the first Christians called the "uncreated light" that is waiting to be unveiled everywhere and in every ordinary thing in creation. This uncreated light discloses the goodness, beauty, and verity instilled in the tree or the owl or the chrysanthemum or the human by God.

This unique illumination—not revealed apart from the cross—is made possible by the profound humility of humanity's incarnate God. The suffering of God in the human flesh of Jesus is what fills the universe with a divine light that is more penetrating than all stars. We begin to see all things in the light of resurrection.

Jesus, "the light of the world," is their hidden light. This light comes from within Jesus and radiates out into the world around him, for Christ is the light of humanity, "the true light, who gives light to everyone" (John 1:9 NLT).

It will be magnificent when we can see this uncreated light shine forth in everything, as in the consummation that John the elder describes as the new Jerusalem: "The city has no need of sun or moon to shine on it, for the glory of God is its light, and its lamp is the Lamb" (Rev. 21:23).

In his book *Hallucinations*, Oliver Sacks recalls a foolish experiment with a combination of mind-altering substances while he was a medical student in New York.[2] While tripping, he asked to see the color indigo, and a blob of indigo appeared for a moment on a wall and then disappeared.

The color stole his heart. Sacks recalls a lifelong search—leafing through the pages of art books, overturning stones, visiting art museums—to see that color again. Sacks muses that perhaps this indigo was once present in creation but is now no longer visible. He felt the color was still there but just beyond his unaided faculties to see it. Listening to Sacks, we can imagine all the original color we are not seeing—and all the color yet to be revealed when all things are transfigured.

G. K. Chesterton was right: The secret of all things is that we have only ever seen, as it were, the back of the world: "That is not a tree, but the back of a tree. That is not a cloud, but the back of a cloud. Cannot you see that everything is stooping and hiding a face? If we could only get round in front."[3]

Peter did get round in front, for a moment, at the peak of that mountain. He saw the face and he saw the light.

The uncreated light is the light that shines from the face of Moses, that envelopes the chariots of fire that carry Elijah beyond the sight of Elisha. Our Father "has made this light shine in our hearts so we could know the glory of God that is seen in the face of Jesus Christ" (2 Cor. 4:6 NLT).

From this human and divine face, shining like the sun in full strength, everything in creation will in the end be transfigured by the uncreated light Peter somehow saw, a consuming fire that reveals the true essence of all things—and redeems further still, well beyond all original created goodness—heals from every participation in evil, and elevates us to participation in the divine nature.

But we do not have to wait until the end to live by this light.

We spend a lot of time in the church teaching folks how to live well in this world on its terms and by its means, when we should teach humans how to live in this world on the terms and by the means of the world that is in the end coming to this world, the end when all things are illumined by the Lamb.

For example, we look at nature and see that the "strongest" survive and so adopt a spiritualized version of how the "fittest" succeed, doing so "Christian-ly," if you will. Yet Isaiah says that in the world God intends, the wolf lies down with the lamb. The nature of the wolf is in the present world *not as it should be.*

Or we assume the female is the "weaker vessel" because "that's the way it's always been" or "that's just how things are," when in the church and in the resurrection there is neither male nor female.

Fallen humans believe that the world operates on a principle of scarcity, that there is not enough to go around for everyone. Watch how often this is the assumption. The gospel trusts the exact opposite: that the world is governed by divine abundance. And we could multiply examples.

By the uncreated light of the resurrection disclosed on the holy mountain, we try to see *through* the present givenness of things to behold the world as God sees the world.

Which has more weight for us: the given (often fallen) reality or the promised transfigured one?

In the world that is coming to this world, there is no future for our armaments. There is no future for our greed. There is no future for our superiority or inferiority complexes. There is no future for unjust scales or for lust. There is no future for cruelty or falsehoods. Humility alone inhabits the future.

When we begin to tell the Christian story well (the Apostles' Creed can help us) and when our Spirit-bearing practices train us in loving other humans and the world as if all things matter more than we can possibly imagine, we begin to trust that a new world is coming to this old world, in which nothing that is not a participation in humility will remain.

When by the courage and charity of Jesus we begin to live amid a distorted nature and among fallen systems as if they are *passing away* and have no future—that the truth of this world is not domination and death but surrender and resurrection—we need the Taboric light that radiates from the face of Christ, the light that converts the way we see the world.

We begin by the Spirit to visit prisoners because we long to see the colors of a transfigured creation. We welcome strangers because we want to hear the praise of trees. We care for the sick because we desire to inhale the aroma of resurrection. We feed the hungry to taste the bread of angels. We clothe the naked to touch the hem of Christ's garment. We give drink to the thirsty to hear the notes that cannot yet be played, to see the light yet hidden from our eyes, to savor the fragrance of forgiveness, to touch the wounds of God, to taste the water of life.

The holy mountain is about the whole creation becoming heaven, about heaven descending to earth, about the difference between heaven and earth coming to an end.

The holy mountain is about the whole creation becoming heaven, about heaven descending to earth, about the difference between heaven and earth coming to an end. It is about a conversation that brings Elijah down from heaven and raises up Moses from the ground, a conversation that brings heaven and earth together in the resurrection, about heaven and earth being charged with the grandeur of God. As Paul says, in the end God will be all in all, thanks to Jesus (1 Cor. 15:28).

The transfiguration shows us that love is a conversation. This conversation invites us (like Peter, with all our misunderstandings, sins, and frailties) into the eternal discussion that is the divine life shared between the Father, Son, and Spirit.

And what is the conversation that Love speaks? What are Moses and Elijah talking about with Jesus?

Love talks always and everywhere about the cross, about the suffering of God in the flesh of Jesus that makes us heirs with the One who has the words of life (John 6:68), words about "the sprinkled blood that speaks a better word than the blood of Abel" (Heb. 12:24).

Graveyards and tombstones are all that we know in this distorted nature we now inhabit, but here on the holy mountain is a sacred conversation that tells us that death dies, that death is trampled down by death, that death is an exodus, a deliverance, a passing through into promise.

The glory on this mountain is in speaking wisely of the cross; it is a conversation about suffering love that heals and does not destroy God or humanity, because love is stronger than death.

CLOUD

As the conversation between Moses, Elijah, and Jesus continues, a light-radiant cloud descends on Mount Tabor. It's the same cloud that descends on Sinai when God signs his law on stone tablets, the pillar of cloud that follows and defends the children of Israel in the wilderness. It's the cloud that fills the temple when the musicians play and sing praise to the God who is good, whose mercy endures forever and ever.

When (as we recalled) Isaiah envisions the Lord ascended on a throne, and the six-wingèd seraph fill the air with their thrice-sung "holies," the interior of the temple is filled with this cloud, like the train of the Lord's billowing robe. This cloud is the Spirit . . . "the spirit of wisdom and understanding, the spirit of counsel and might, the spirit of knowledge and the fear of the Lord" (Isa. 11:2).

And here on Tabor, from deep in the light-radiant cloud, comes the voice of the Father, saying, "This is my Son, marked by my love; *listen to him*" (Matt. 17:5 Message, emphasis added).

Moses and Elijah fade from view, and heeding the Father's voice, we now read their Scriptures in the light that radiates from Jesus and illumines its pages. And when we turn from those pages back to lived life, we see his light in every face we meet.

Moses was told by God that he could not see his face and live. And yet here the disciples see the face of Jesus become "as the sun" and hear the voice of the Father testify of his identity as God's Son as they are enveloped by the Spirit. Our sun does not usually cause us to lose our balance and fall to the ground, but this light and this voice and this cloud overpower the disciples.

Jesus does not leave them on their faces in the dirt. He touches them gently and lifts them up so they are eye to eye, and now they see only Jesus: "For Moses, the law, and Elijah, the prophecy, have become one only in the Gospel of Jesus. They have not remained three as they formerly were, but the three have become one,"[1] as Origen, the third-century Egyptian teacher, says.

The Scriptures are veiled for those who do not begin their experience and witness of God with Mary's son, the One who touches the unclean, with the One rejected for a criminal, this transfigured One who raises the dead and rebuilds the world.

Transfiguration folds time and brings disparate events together, for this is not just a moment between Moses, Elijah, and Jesus, but between the disciples and triune Love. Transfiguration helps us remember that *all* the appearances of God in time, like the (ancient) appearances to Moses and Elijah on Sinai, are but *one* appearance, and so our (present) moment on Tabor participates also in the moment when John encounters Love as a figure walking amid a seven-branched menorah in the opening of the Apocalypse.

In Revelation, Jesus lays his right hand on John—and on every human who has ever lived or ever will live—and this is what Jesus Christ says: "Do not be afraid; I am the First and the Last and the Living One. I was dead, and see, I am alive forever and ever, and I have the keys of Death and of Hades" (Rev. 1:17–18).

Transfiguration reveals Jesus as the human God intends from the beginning, and Jesus is the truest self of every human. This is the mystery to which Paul bears witness: "I am crucified with Christ, nevertheless I live" (Gal. 2:20 KJV).

Pride is not your truest self; humility is what you were made to embody. Hate is not the essence of your person; love is what you forever are. Every human is made in the image of shalom, for Peace is another name for God. A desire for peace is the natural disposition of any human, and yet we are often breakers of peace rather than makers of it.

Transfiguration reveals Jesus as the human God intends from the beginning, and Jesus is the truest self of every human.

Childhood trauma; the history and experience of family, tribe, and nation; belligerent influencers; angelic evil; our own willful choices; and mental or spiritual brokenness can lead some humans to embrace violence, to become fanatical enactors of unimaginable harm.

Because Jesus Christ is our origin, the true nature of every human is nonviolence and forbearance and charity, but we suffer from horrific amnesia and find ourselves embedded in worlds that are overrun with often unchecked malevolent powers.

Prayer is joining Jesus Christ in the work of helping humans remember who they are. Joining Christ in giving ourselves in love for the world can help break this spell of forgetting, this odor of death, that hangs over our violence. Despite what our myths sometimes suggest, violence cannot heal the amnesia that afflicts those who bring violence. Only Love can help us remember who we are as icons of Love.

Just before we get to Tabor, Peter is shocked when Jesus tells the disciples that he's going to Jerusalem to die, because for Peter their story is not supposed to end with Jesus dead. Maybe it is Peter's affection for Jesus or sheer passion for his friend that makes him shout that this can never happen, that Jesus cannot allow himself to be killed.

Who would want to be parted from Jesus? We would want him to keep overturning tables and healing the sick and freeing prisoners and raising the dead until the whole world was well, everything pieced back together.

Jesus decides he must make it clear to Peter and to us that any suggestion that Jesus has *not* come to lay down his life as God and as man for the life of the world is so out of touch with his mission as to be demonic.

Jesus gathers everyone together and describes how the world works, describes the way the life that is God works, and it opposes all fallen human intuition: To be alive forever, you must lay down your life; for the world to live, God must die. Jesus tells us that unless we yield to his way of selflessness, we will be embarrassed when the human God returns with all the holy angels.

Some think Jesus will return at the end of this world as we now know it as a bloodthirsty conqueror who puts the conquerors of history to shame, as an alien force that wields limitless destructive capacity. They think we will fall to our knees because his presence will so terrify us with paralytic fear that we will wish we were dead.

Yet Christians trust that God does not change. The same Jesus who washes feet, and welcomes children, and dies with criminals is the same Jesus who comes at the end of the world in all the glory and majesty of his unmatched humility. "Every knee will bow—in heaven and on earth and under the earth—and every tongue confess that Jesus Christ is Lord to the glory of the Father" (Phil. 2:10–11 NET). This is true not because God is coercive but because the unfettered revelation of God as Love will buckle our knees.

It is the vision of divine humility found in Jesus that will embarrass us with its riches if instead of choosing the way of surrender, we chose the way of hubris, the way of personal empire, our own way.

If we have grabbed at every morsel of our paltry life and hoarded it with a deathlike grip, if when Jesus returns we are self-absorbed, we will want to hide from the gaze of self-forgetting, blood-stained Love. And he tells us these things as a warning because he loves us and wants us to enter life. We have walked away from the eternal conversation about love. God becomes human to draw us back into the conversation between Moses, Elijah, and Jesus about the Tree of Life.

As Karl Barth intuited, the finished work of Jesus Christ is the only true change that has occurred or ever will occur in any human (or in humanity as a species), and his is the change in humanity that makes the difference for us all.[2] Indeed, mysteriously, as we have seen, it is not so much a change in humanity as that Jesus nailed to the tree is revealed as humanity's *original and final constitution*, for surrounded by the light of Tabor, we see what it is for any of us to be a creature at all.

Paul reminds us that we are the body of Christ that is transfigured on the mountain because we are made one body with him by the Spirit: "All of us, with unveiled faces, seeing the glory of the Lord as though reflected in a mirror, are being transformed into the same image from one degree of glory to another, for this comes from the Lord, the Spirit" (2 Cor. 3:18). We reflect and become what we behold when we see the face of God in the human Jesus, a face streaked with tears.

LAZARUS

In his Gospel, John tells us there are many stories about Jesus he leaves out. He says the world could not contain all the books that could be written. And that is not hyperbole; every story in all the libraries of the world that offers forgiveness or healing or justice or deliverance or mercy or truth is about Christ. Jesus is the Lord of every story.

The raising of Lazarus (John 11:1–44) is a Gospel moment that tells the entire scriptural story of God and humanity and the world.

We are told that Lazarus is sick. And we are told that Jesus loves Lazarus. It's important that we know both of those things. We are sick with death. And God loves us, even in our illness.

"Lord, he whom you love is ill," Mary and Martha tell Jesus (John 11:3). He has contracted the same disease that infects us all. And just as in Genesis, we who are dying, separated from the God who made us from nothing for the sake of love alone, are given the same promise as Mary and Martha: "This illness does not lead to death; rather, it is for God's glory, so that the Son of God may be glorified through it" (11:4).

Genesis tells us the Son of Eve will crush the head of the serpent, the source of death, his final enemy; he will trample the snake who seeks to destroy us.

God in Jesus Christ will draw near to Jerusalem—will approach danger and death, will put himself in harm's way, will take a great risk—to save Lazarus. God wills to venture God's very life: "Rabbi, the Jewish leaders were just now trying to stone you! Are you going there again?" (John 11:8 NET).

While the disciples think Lazarus is in bed, resting from an illness, and conclude there's no earthly reason for their rabbi to risk so much, Jesus is serious. He always is when he's talking about death. He knows the reality of our situation. He knows we are dying. He knows Lazarus is dead.

In this Gospel story, there is also the great mystery of God's inexplicable waiting in the face of death. Jesus does not go immediately to Bethany to see Lazarus. God knows Lazarus is dying, and yet he lingers. When Jesus finally arrives, Lazarus has been dead four days.

This is not news to us. So many have died. And so many are dying. He knows we are dying. And so many are still waiting, hoping for God.

Israel waited for centuries for the Messiah. And we wait, for we are with them one synagogue. The world waits. We wait in all the cemeteries of the world, and beside every tomb as well as every altar. We hope, and we doubt, and we grieve, and we cry. But we do not cry or wait or grieve alone.

But I am getting ahead of the story John tells. We must wait some more.

Before we get to the tomb of Lazarus, we must meet Jesus on the road. And in the figure of Martha, we hear our own grief and perplexity in the face of death: "Lord, if you had been here, my brother would not have died" (John 11:21).

Where were you? What took you so long? Didn't you know we needed you? If only you had been here! These are the things we say at the graves of our loved ones, in the destruction and death that overtake our lives, in the catastrophes as well as the ordinary course of most days.

And yet what an astonishing reply Martha receives. It reveals the character of God and the character of the new humanity that is present among us in Jesus: "I am the resurrection and the life. Those who believe in me, even though they die, will live, and everyone who lives and believes in me will never die. Do you believe this?" (John 11:25–26).

This is not just God's question for Martha. This is the question our lives pose to us. Do we trust in the face of our collective illness amid a broken world that Jesus Christ is life and resurrection? Can we reply as Martha replies? "Yes, Lord, I believe that you are the Messiah, the Son of God, the one coming into the world" (John 11:27). Martha voices this Spirit-enabled response to the startling declaration of Jesus, and by the same Spirit we join her.

As difficult and trying as almost all of life is, we have hope in the middle of a fragile and grief-stricken world because we do not wait alone. We wait with God. We wait with a God who weeps with us as one of us.

"Jesus began to weep" (John 11:35).

I imagine that Christ stood there by the tomb of Lazarus and sobbed. This is not only Jesus the human friend of Lazarus who on many occasions enjoyed laughter and wine and late-night conversation with his companion-of-the-heart; this is Jesus, the God who made Lazarus, who loves Lazarus. This is the divine person who loves us humanly and the human person who loves us divinely.

This story about Lazarus reveals God's radical identification with death-bound humanity, personified in Mary and Martha and Lazarus, those whom Christ loves.

Christ Jesus loves every human. He weeps with us at the tombs of our beloved dead. And he not only cries. He is angry. And that is a very good thing to remember: that in the sharpness of our despair, when with the psalmist we cry out from the depths, the human God joins us in our prayer, as we join the prayer he first inspired in the heart of the Spirit-bearing chief musician:

> Help, GOD—I've hit rock bottom!
>   Master, hear my cry for help!
> Listen hard! Open your ears!
>   Listen to my cries for mercy.
> If you, GOD, kept records on wrongdoings,
>   who would stand a chance?
> As it turns out, forgiveness is your habit,
>   and that's why you're worshiped.
> I pray to GOD—my life a prayer—
>   and wait for what he'll say and do. (Ps. 130:1–5 Message)

As Jesus waits with us at the tombs of all our silenced loves, waits with all who are six feet under, he is deeply troubled. Christ is angry but not at Lazarus or his mourners or any of his human brothers or sisters. Christ's anger is directed at God's enemies: death, hell, and the grave. Anger at human death is one of the deepest forms of solidarity with the God who is human.

We find ourselves standing with the mourners, and with the human God, by the simple cave cut out of the hillside in Bethany, and a heavy stone has been rolled against it. And Lazarus has been dead four days—in the tomb one day longer than the body of Jesus—and he stinks because death reeks.

Yes, Jesus stands with us by the grave of Lazarus, and by every tomb—the ones still marked by stones, the ones we visit from time to time, as well as the countless burial grounds that are lost to the decay of time. Jesus lies in every seed of buried humanity, in every corpse that lies moldering in the ground.

Then in our grief and from the heart of the God who grieves, we hear the divine voice of the Lamb slain before the foundation of the world, the human voice of the Word that in the beginning spoke the worlds into being from nothing. With the stain and sting of tears still on his divine and human face, he shouts, "Lazarus, come out!" And together with Lazarus all persons hear the voice that calls us back into being forever.

Jesus says, "Unbind him, and let him go" (John 11:44), and his words are a universal declaration. The resurrection word to Lazarus is also our resurrection word. Jesus takes from us all the grave clothes that bind us to death.

Together with Lazarus all persons hear the voice that calls us back into being forever.

And it does not matter if our bones have become dust swirling in a valley or silt at the bottom of the ocean or if there's not one trace of our DNA to be discovered. His love can call us back to life from nothing.

He remembers our dismembered bodies and brings back all that makes us the sort of people we are. And this includes also the traumas and harms that happen to us, somehow cleansed, as his wounds are, of anything that might continue to pain or limit us.

After all, we are only the sorts of people we are, people who respond to the world and others and events in the ways we do, not only by innate gifts, intuitions, and attributes, but by the hurts and tragedies we have experienced. I am the sort of person I am and no other because I lived through the death of my father.

When we are raised from death we are not lobotomized but cured, still the persons whom those who love us remember but in whom every experience that makes us who we are is transfigured into wisdom and empathy for our good and the good of the kingdom of heaven. Every person we were—the child, the teenager, the early adult, the mid-lifer, the aging self—is in the end present and united, rescued and integrated.

If we trust God makes the world and us from nothing, and if we trust God can resurrect us and the world from almost next to nothing—reconstituting the complexity of every person, body and soul, from death—then there is no imprisoned will that cannot be released, no hard heart that cannot be softened, no corrupt mind that cannot be made clean.

If I had the time and the energy and the skill, and lots of humans helping me, I could quarry a new tomb out of the side of a hill of rock, but I cannot bring even one person back from the dead. None of us can. This is why in the end the world and we humans can be redeemed and rectified and made well only by Love.

All *will* be made well. I don't know how God makes all things well, but I trust that Jesus *can* and that Jesus *will*. Listen to Ezekiel:

> Mortal, these bones are the whole house of Israel. They say, "Our bones are dried up, and our hope is lost; we are cut off completely." Therefore prophesy and say to them: Thus says the Lord God: I am going to open your graves and bring you up from your graves, O my people, and I will bring you back to the land of Israel. And you shall know that I am the Lord when I open your graves and bring you up from your graves, O my people. I will put my spirit within you, and you shall live, and I will place you on your own soil; then you shall know that I, the Lord, have spoken and will act. (Ezek. 37:11–14)

Because of what Jesus did in raising Lazarus from the dead, many believe in him. When the Pharisees hear about the effect Jesus and the resurrected Lazarus are having on folks, they plot to kill Jesus and Lazarus.

Jesus withdraws for a brief time into the wilderness but returns to Bethany six days before the Passover, where a dinner has been prepared in Christ's honor by Martha and Mary.

One of the persons at table, their brother Lazarus, is seated with Jesus and the others, having returned from the place of the dead because the cross makes resurrection available to every moment of time.

Mary commits a wildly intimate, vulnerable, and memorable act, in any age or culture: she anoints the feet of Jesus with perfume and wipes his feet with her hair. The color of the anointing fragrance, a spikenard from the north of India, is deep red, red like a rose on a thorn bush, precious and expensive, and its incense fills the air.

Mary is awake and understands the moment. She knows where Jesus is going; he's going to die. She is already in mourning. Mary is preparing him, Jesus tells us, for burial.

They are all seated there in Bethany—and we are seated with them—in the kingdom of heaven. We inhale the fragrance of Christ, red with his bloody anointing. Christ is, we are, the aroma of resurrection in the world, as it continues to overthrow anything that opposes love.

And now we've arrived at what the older traditions—and more and more contemporary Christ followers—call Holy Week. Matthew and John give us the deepest accounts of this week. We will tell parts of their gospel as well as we are able because this week in Jerusalem cannot possibly matter more.

JERUSALEM

The coin is small and plated in silver. A denarius weighs about 3.9 grams, less than an American nickel. A laborer in Galilee earns one at day's end, and you need one to pay the Roman head tax.

When his opponents ask Jesus whether anyone should pay the tax (Matt. 22:15–22), Jesus sees through their mischief: A yes angers those resisting Rome; a no aligns him with the resistance. He asks to see the coin for the tax.

There is an imperial mint in the new tribute city that Herod built in Tiberius, and the coin they show Jesus might have been minted there. On the coin's face, the profile of Tiberius Caesar, the Roman emperor, has been struck along with an inscription that reads, "Caesar Augustus Tiberius, son of the divine Augustus."

They show Jesus the denarius, a coin they should not possess—Jesus, notably, does not have one on him—because its face and inscription make it an idol, forbidden in the temple precincts where they are standing.

Jesus asks whose image and inscription are on the face of the coin. They answer, "Caesar's." Jesus replies, "Give therefore to Caesar the things that are Caesar's and to God the things that are God's" (Matt. 22:21).

The word for "image" Jesus uses is *eikōn*. Jesus is returning to Genesis 1, where we are told that humans are made in the image (*eikōn*) of God.

The coin bears the image of Caesar, is minted by him. If he wants it, pay it back to him, Jesus says. But all humans bear the stamp of God, belong to God, so give your whole self to God.

Jesus is concerned not with the tax or the coin but with announcing the true identity of every human, with calling us to our creation in the divine image and to the death we all must die. The express image of God pressed into clay is Jesus Christ, and as John Behr says, Jesus "has shown us what it is to be God in the way he dies as a human being."[1]

The coin is an idol, something that has no actual life, is unable to give life, with only a pretense to power. But humans are not idols. We are called to give life as God gives life by giving ourselves.

"The glory of God is a living human being,"[2] writes Irenaeus, and this "living human being" is for the first Christians the person who freely gives oneself for the life of the world: the martyr.

The path Jesus treads to the cross is the path all humans follow to become human. The passion of Jesus is the end to which all human lives are aimed by God like an arrow.

Two days before this exchange about the coin, on a Sunday, Jesus journeys to Jerusalem from Bethpage, a nearby village, mounting a borrowed young donkey and its donkey mother.

Jesus is not the only divine image bearer coming into Jerusalem. Pilgrims from all over the world are arriving for the annual Passover. There were normally about 30,000 people in Jerusalem, but now there are at least 180,000.

A crowd accompanies Jesus on foot, going ahead of him and following behind. They are largely Galileans from the north. They begin to throw their garments along the road. They cut palm branches, which they wave in the air while shouting a praise from Psalm 118: "Blessed is the one who comes in the name of the LORD" (v. 26).

The crowd's devotion and praise identify Jesus with Israel's promised Messiah, and this time Jesus does not stop them or make himself hidden. He seems to want to be conspicuous, knows this Galilean throng parading into the city and shouting praises will draw out the Judaean residents of the city.

The exulting pilgrims hope for someone like Judas of Galilee, who'd led a revolt when Jesus was a child. Or perhaps someone like the sons of Mattathias Maccabee, who nearly two hundred years before had freed Israel from the Seleucid Empire by violence, only to eventually be conquered by the Romans.

The human who rides into Jerusalem to die, the God who approaches Jerusalem's eastern gate on an ass is not arriving to lead an armed resistance. Jesus rides a donkey and not a war horse. He has no sword but the sword that issues from his mouth in words of life. His sword does not kill but grants life without end. He rides a donkey to fulfill the prophecy of Zechariah:

> Rejoice greatly, O daughter Zion!
>   Shout aloud, O daughter Jerusalem!
> See, your king comes to you;
>   triumphant and victorious is he,
> humble and riding on a donkey,
>   on a colt, the foal of a donkey. (9:9)

Jesus imitates his father David, who rode into Jerusalem meekly, in great sorrow and humility, after the bitter loss of his son Absalom. Jesus is riding a donkey as a child, like Solomon did to his coronation. He is riding into the city as Judah rode in Genesis 49:10–11, his colt and donkey awaiting him bound to vines, his robes washed in the blood of grapes, in his own blood and not the blood of others.

The Galilean crowd extols and lauds Jesus but does not see in Jesus the Lamb slain to bring an end to killing as the means of salvation.

Jesus is leading them not to the Jerusalem with walls, fortified against violence by an always-superior violence, but to the Jerusalem that comes down from heaven, whose gates are always open to all nations. He is leading them to a city where we learn not to make war anymore, what Bede the Venerable calls "the kingdom of the gentle."[3]

Jesus is leading them not to the Jerusalem with walls . . . but to the Jerusalem that comes down from heaven, whose gates are always open to all nations.

Jesus is not like the kings of the past. He is gentle and lowly of heart. He is the Prince of Peace come to cast out the prince of this world, the prince of bloodshed, by being lifted up so all humans can be drawn to his shalom.

As Jesus ascends to the gates of Jerusalem surrounded by the palm-waving crowd eager for the overthrow of usurping pagans, Jesus can see off in the distance the wilderness of Judaea. Does he recall in this moment how satan had offered him there all that is his in all the kingdoms of the world in all times and places?

In that wilderness, satan said, "All of this can be yours," and attempted to shift the Son's devotion from the greatest possible gift—his union with the Father, who gives *all things* to us with himself—to mere temporal possession of the shadows of the good satan promises to us apart from God.

Satan "ascends" to the nothing he possesses under his own fallen power, as our first ancestors were tempted by him to do and did, by grasping for equality with God. Christ shows us that we descend in and with the Father's love, even into hell, in order to ascend.

Jesus rejected satan's final wilderness temptation, and he puts satan behind him once again as he turns his head back toward the approaching city gate. Jesus has set his face like a flint toward suffering, and he trusts beyond all the coming brutal shaming that he will not be ashamed.

Jesus looks down at his feet. Perhaps he remembers how Mary anointed them with expensive perfume and wiped them with her hair the night before. The beast of burden he rides has kept his feet clean, and the aroma of forgiveness that filled the room in Bethany is still fragrant in the air.

Near the gates, the people of the city and its leaders are coming out to see what's happening. They ask the Galilean pilgrims what on earth this commotion is about. They answer that Jesus is the prophet from Nazareth, from Galilee—which is, unlike Judaea, under Herodian, not Roman, rule.

The city dwellers are not ready for a rabble of country folk to cause trouble with the Roman garrison, to disrupt their compromise with wealth and power, but the pilgrim crowd is enthusiastic, ready for anything.

As John reports, the anxious leaders of Jerusalem see that the "whole world" has now gone after Jesus and decide to kill him (John 12:19). Some Greeks arrive, telling Philip they want to see Jesus, and Philip takes them. And seeing the gentiles arrive, Jesus knows his "hour" has come. The Son of Man is about to be glorified.

From the city gate, Jesus enters the nearby temple complex, the center of Jewish national identity. Jesus gets angry about merchants at rows of tables in the courtyard, selling access to God and his mercies. He fashions a whip from basket-weaving materials, from reeds, to drive out the money changers. It's not the sort of whip that will in a few days cut deep gashes into the back of Jesus or later scar Paul and others tortured for Christ's sake. It's more like a brush or broom, made for dispersing livestock—not for harm.

God's zealous desire that his temple be a house of prayer for *all nations*, a sacred place of contemplation and quiet within the world, is disturbed by the chaos and greed of a trading floor. The temple is corrupted by those bartering in the forgiveness of God as at a market—salvation as transaction, not gift—and at the expense of the poor, who came to make sacrifices. And Jesus cannot stand this or let it stand.

It is a great good to have a God who has wrath for our wrongdoing (who is not grateful that child abuse angers God?), but that same wrath in us is precarious—a very fragile and dangerous thing. Human anger does not produce the righteousness God seeks, especially when the humans in question imagine they are channels for the righteous anger or judgment that belongs to God alone. We are not usually capable of turning over tables without egos or agendas. Jesus turned over tables to make space for prayer, not to prove a point.

What a thin reed we grasp when we use this temple story to give endless permission to our anger and avarice. We hang so much on so little. We literally grasp at straws when we use this cord of wicker Christ fashioned to support our violence, when the cross—the destruction of the temple of Jesus's body by Rome's vicious whips—is a renunciation of all human violence, of violence itself.

God isn't like the hypocritical parent who demands we ignore what he does and do what he says. Rather, his holy commands for us—like "Do not kill"—are descriptions of his very essence as God. Killing a divine image bearer is so at odds with the grain of the universe that the spilt blood of any and every human has a unique property: It cries out to God for reckoning.

The morning after the cleansing of the temple, walking back into Jerusalem, Jesus tries to gather some breakfast from a roadside fig tree. The tree is fruitless but full of leaves. It withers in moments when Jesus curses it.

The only part of the good creation that Jesus destroys in the Gospels is this fig tree. In Genesis, fig leaves are a sign of our ancestors' shame, of a false perception that all differences—uncreated and created, heaven and earth, male and female—are now divisions and competitions instead of inherent unities. In this unfruitful fig tree, Jesus curses our shame and our discord.

Christ is the good fig tree that bears fruit in the third year. The leaves of his cross will heal nations (Rev. 22:2) and produce the fruit of repentance that brings reconciliation to all things.

That evening, looking out on Jerusalem, Jesus mourns the city he will give his life for, mourns that its inhabitants are asleep to the things that lead to peace, mourns that she will soon lie in ruins again. Jesus remembers the many exiled of Jerusalem's past and the great exile that is coming—how in just four decades not one of the temple stones will be left on stone. As he grieves, it is no stretch to imagine that he prays.

Psalm 147 is written from exile, as Jerusalem lies derelict, her culture dead, her people scattered. Even so the psalmist trusts—beyond any tangible hope—that her refugees will be regathered, their broken hearts mended, their wounds healed. Jesus is this psalmist's star-namer and raven-feeder who on this evening dons sackcloth and ashes to sit shiva for Jerusalem.

When my youngest daughter was in middle school, we attended a winter choral concert in which her choir performed a song in Hebrew, "Ani Ma'amin," composed by Azriel David

Fastag, a Modzizter Hasidic Jew who died at Treblinka concentration camp.

The melody is in a gorgeous minor key, and the choir was accompanied by an exceptional young Chinese violinist and by piano. I was moved to tears by its beauty and sensed something very profound in the room as the song was performed, even though I did not understand the words.

Then, during a pause in the song, three of the girls left the choir and from a lone microphone at the front of the stage read the following explanation of the song's origin: "'Ani Ma'amin' gained its greatest significance during the Holocaust. Thousands of Jews entered the gas chambers singing this very song, proclaiming allegiance to God to their last breath. Eyewitness accounts tell us that the music would decrescendo to silence only as the gas choked the singers."

This is a translation of the lyrics: "I believe in God, in a greater truth, and in things greater than this world in spite of all that has happened. I believe that the Messiah will come, and he will find me waiting. No matter how long he tarries, no matter how long he delays his coming, I will continue to believe. No matter what the future holds, I believe."[4]

I hope you trust that the God who hangs from the tree for all nations never abandons anyone in death, that people who have the melody of this song on their lips as they march with faith into their tomb, driven into the poison chambers mostly by baptized Christians, are martyrs. The Christ we know in the opening of the Scriptures and the breaking of the bread has in his bosom every one of these lambs led to the slaughter.

SUPPER

On the evening before he dies, Jesus gathers his followers for a Passover meal at the end of the world.

At the table prepared in the upper room, in the presence of humanity's enemies—disease, famine, pestilence, violence, and death—it is Christ's death as the Passover Lamb that is received in the meal that he offers. Today when we eat the bread he blesses and breaks and drink the cup he offers, we are preaching the death of Christ. We eat and drink the death of Christ, and by his death alone, we have life.

As Jesus taught in Galilee the year before, on this last night in Jerusalem, the followers of Christ, and all those who follow Christ after, are eating "the flesh of the Son of Man," are drinking "his blood" (John 6:53), and whoever eats this bread and drinks this cup lives forever.

As bread and wine become by the Spirit the body and blood of Jesus, a bloodless sacrifice that is all gift, we are touched, as we have said, by the fire of Love taken with tongs from the altar and placed on our lips.

Whenever we eat this meal, Christ's dying is given to us as our living. For the Eucharist is God's human and divine life made sharable, made livable, a living made possible by dying as Christ died, by being united to him on the cross, by becoming together with Christ the body and blood, spirit and life.

God desires to be in union with humans, considers us such suitable vessels for the divine presence that Jesus gives us this meal so that in partaking of bread and wine that are Christ ascended and descended, we together become Christ, become the Father's, become by the Spirit christs.

The Eucharist is the divine and human nutrition we need to become as permanent as Love—partakers of the divine nature—by joining the passion of Jesus Christ. As our teacher Nicholas Cabasilas shares, "Since it was not possible for us to ascend to him and participate in that which is his, he came down to us and partook of that which is ours. . . . As we partake of his human body and blood, we receive God himself into our souls. It is thus God's body and blood which we receive, his soul, mind, and will, no less than those of his humanity."[1]

Our Lord is gifted to us in the Scriptures and in the Eucharist; his life sustains us in those words, audible and edible. This is why the second-century pastor Ignatius trusted he would become in his death "a word of God," and "pure bread for Christ," and finally, "a human being."[2] God is apt to dwell in us as us and to make us together by this meal the actual body of Christ in the world.

The words Jesus speaks at this last supper—among them that we are to love everyone by the standard of human love Jesus embodies, that Jesus will remain human and stay with all humans until the end of the world, that the peace of Christ is available to every human even in the hardest things—are ratified by the response of Jesus to Philip's question at the table.

Philip asks Jesus to show them the Father, and Jesus wonders aloud how Philip could have lived with Jesus all this time and not know that Jesus and the Father are one, that to see Jesus is to see the invisible God, that there is no God behind Jesus, that to love as Jesus loves us is to love as God loves.

The rituals of holy Thursday, when liturgical churches relive the events of the Last Supper—washing feet, setting a table, praying, eating and drinking Christ—are about ordinary love. There is nothing hip about the practices. When you take off your shoes and let someone clean your heels, all cool, all control, whatever distance we like to keep go out the window.

Theophilus of Alexandria tells us that our Lord "clothed with light . . . girds himself with a towel; he who gathers the waters of the seas . . . pours water in a bowl; he who measured heaven with his hand's span and holds the earth in his grasp"[3] takes the feet of his friends into his hands and makes them clean, and so on this night, we who are Christ wash Christ's feet.

The Spirit meets us in this quiet serving. No one stands out. Talent is unimportant. Love makes itself nothing, makes itself of no account, for love of the world. The human God serves, and we want to be human as God is human, and so by grace we serve.

Though the Gospels give only glimpses, it is my theory that Jesus is an *actual servant* among the disciples. Yes, he serves by healing and delivering and setting free but also by washing and folding clothes and keeping whatever needs fixing in repair. Jesus sets tables, cooks a breakfast of fish on charcoal, mends their ropes. He lives the same childlike life he lived as a child, doing all the domestic things for Mary and all the apprentice things for Joseph.

Before their journey to Jerusalem, Jesus notices the disciples arguing about who of them is greatest. He tells them the greatest among them is the servant of all, and he places a child among them and tells them they must be like children.

James and John ask Jesus if they can sit at his right and at his left when he comes into his "glory." They do not know that providence has assigned this honor to criminals, that the human

God's throne is a cross, that this God would rather be executed with the convicted than wield power in the ways that those who execute them do.

Jesus gathers the quarrelsome disciples together, wounded—as we all are—by desire for the ring of power, and makes them a promise: "This is not the way it will be with you." Jesus promises we will live differently than the way of manipulation and coercion, and he is the One who invokes without coercion that different living in each of us.

After the Passover meal and foot washing, Jesus walks out into the night with his friends to a garden called Gethsemane, an olive grove across the Kidron Valley on a slope overlooking Jerusalem. Jesus goes there to pray and invites Peter, James, and John, the same disciples who were with him on Mount Tabor, to pray with him.

His disciples cannot stay awake.

The Son is in great sorrow and anguish as he converses with the Father. He is not playacting. Jesus truly suffers anxiety. He sweats and cries out as he faces down not just his death but all our deaths. But he does not suffer any of this as we do, is not changed by these physical and emotional terrors. He transforms them so that we can endure our own nights of anguish, our own pain, our own death.

Robert Jenson says, "He does not suffer the fact that he suffers."[4] Cyril of Alexandria helps us here:

> If he had not been afraid, our nature would not have been freed from fear. If he had not grieved, there could never have been any deliverance from grief. If he had not been troubled and alarmed, there would have been no escape from these conditions. For every human experience, you will find the same corresponding

> experience in Christ. The passions of his flesh are stirred up, however, not to overcome him as they do us, but so that once they are stirred up they may be destroyed by the power of the Word who dwells in the flesh, transforming our nature to a better condition.[5]

Gethsemane is a place to linger with the Word made flesh. Many of our greatest teachers discern something deep and inexpressible at work and bear witness to the mystery they encounter there, Hippolytus among them:

> Although he was God clearly revealed, he did not disown what was human about himself as well. He is hungry and exhausted, weary and thirsty; he fears and flees and is troubled when he prays. He sleeps on a pillow, yet as God he has a nature that does not know sleeping. He asks to be excused the suffering of the cup, yet he was present in the world for this very reason. In his agony, he sweats and an angel strengthens him, yet he strengthens those who believe in him and has taught them by his example to treat death with contempt.[6]

About a decade before he died, while kneeling in the crypt of a church in Rome, my stepfather had a vision of Jesus. He said that a wall in front of him became translucent and that through the wall he could see into a garden. Jesus was there, on his knees, his robes stained with mud from kneeling. And he was praying.

After a while he asked Jesus why he was kneeling in the mud, and Jesus said, "This is where I always am, praying for the world."

Dad was a bit of a mystic and had several unusual experiences of the divine, but this one rings the most authentic. The human who is God prays for us always, prays for all of us, for the world.

When one of us is God and is the One who *always* prays for us, we start to glimpse something: God knows what it's like to be in our skin. This is not Christ's memory of a time and place in the distant past but something he always bears, always feels in eternity.

Jesus remembers what it's like to feel alone, even in a large gathering. Jesus knows what it's like to be betrayed by a friend, to be laughed at for his differences and mocked. He remembers the embrace of his mother. He was and is one of us who is *for* us.

Jesus still knows what it's like to be human because he *remains* one of us—the human for humans. His hands in eternity are human hands.

When we join our hands in prayer, as some folks do when they pray, I wonder: Does Jesus also join his hands in prayer? We know that his hands still bear the scars of the wounds we gave him as he sought to love us. I imagine that as he prays for us, he runs his thumbs over the scars on his hands. Jesus still knows what it's like to be human because he *remains* one of us—the human for humans. His hands in eternity are human hands.

Suddenly, the quiet garden is filled with torch light and an armed party. One of the friends of Jesus has betrayed Jesus to Jerusalem's leaders for a price, and a cheap one at that. Judas values twelve ounces of perfume Mary used to anoint Jesus (worth three hundred silver pieces) over the human God. Judas trades Jesus in for just thirty pieces!

Jesus had washed Judas's feet, feet he knew would run to betray him. Jesus had fed Judas his own body, the body he would give up to the arresting party. Yet after Judas's kiss of betrayal, Jesus calls Judas "my friend," calls him by name, calls him back to himself.

Judas repents, makes restitution, and in deathly despair hangs himself. There is no greater poverty than to be convinced that the only answer is to take your own life, yet God remains with the poor. God does not abandon us in our poverties. God does not abandon Judas. He is among the party who did "not know what they were doing" (Luke 23:34), and with his next-to-last breath Jesus pardons all who plot against him.

Peter grabs a sword to stop anyone from taking Jesus, the One who has the words of life, away from him. In his haste and fear, Peter cuts off Malchus's ear, but Jesus heals Malchus's ear so he can hear the gospel. The One who forms all things human can put anything back together with the touch of his hand, and when the entire arresting party falls to the ground, Jesus raises them up and lets them take him. Then God is led away into the night in handcuffs.

The mind that is in Christ Jesus is a gift. It is given to us. It is not grasped or wrested by force. What is this "mind" that is by grace already ours in Jesus Christ? It is extreme humility and it leads to the cross. Humility is not violent or coercive. It does not seek its own. It is without jealousy or envy. It does not grasp or take but gives itself in trust.

I trust Jesus because he rides into Jerusalem on a donkey, forsaking the kingdoms of this world, forsaking the sword, unwilling that anyone should be slain so that he might rule or have his way. His way is not the way of history. His way is not the way of our moment in time or of any moment in time. His mind is not "just give me what I want, and no one gets hurt." Jesus defies all expectations about God. And this is why I trust Jesus as God.

We learn from the human life Jesus led what it means to be God in eternity, and we learn from the sort of God Jesus is what it means to be human, and what stands out in all of this is humility. Humility rides into Jerusalem. Humility is arrested. Humility is cursed. Humility is beaten. Humility is crucified. Humility is buried.

In 2004, a film premiered during Lent. The film depicts the week leading up to Jesus's cross. There's a scene in the film of Jesus falling flat on his face into a dusty road. As he is surrounded by crowds, a crown of thorns on his head, the heavy timber Jesus is carrying on his shoulder comes down hard on his back.

When Jesus hits the ground just yards from her, Mary flashes back to a moment when as a child Jesus stumbled and hurt himself. In her memory, Jesus runs to her in pain, and she takes him into her arms of comfort. Startled back from her vision—back to the reality of her son lying prostrate in the dust—Mary springs to life and rushes to Christ's aid.

When Jesus sees her, he shoulders his cross once again, and as he slowly rises back to his feet, he meets Mary's face, looks into her eyes, and says, "Behold, Mother, I make all things new."[7]

This is how God makes all things new: not by waving a magic wand, not by taking up a sword or dropping a bomb, not by making himself a tyrant, like so many tyrants in history who convince themselves that they are doing good when they are doing evil, but by dying in the most shameful way imaginable.

Jesus is different in every way from what we have thought of God, more truly different than anything or anyone has differed from anything or anyone else. Jesus Christ is the image of the invisible God, bearing the very impress of his nature: Jesus is lowly, poor, naked, and humiliated, beaten and spat upon, whipped and crucified.

But in Jesus all this lowliness is how authentic divine strength is made known. Chris Green says it well: "Jesus' weakness was not, needless to say, a form of depravity or lifelessness. His humanity was not pale, but radiant. He was not fainthearted or spineless. He did not live in apprehension and anxiety any more than he lived in anger and immodesty. In the way that he suffered and died, he perfected human weakness, exposing every power that pretends to be the source and goal of life."[8]

Only this God can save, but he saves precisely as this human, and we are not human until we are human as God is human. The cross is the divine measure of any authentic humanity.

CROSS

God makes what he loves and loves what he makes, and when we fall away from the Love God is, God becomes what he makes to make what he loves permanent. This is the world's story.

There is a simplicity in the cross that we sometimes mar with too many words, with theories that keep us from awe and repentance. We will try to avoid that here.

Our God is the God who is willing to submit all of God to our violence and to death for the sake of the love they forever are, for our sake, for love of the image of God in humanity, for love of the good creation. He is willing to die to cause the sickness of death to vanish from human nature like straw in flame, to deliver the cosmos from impermanence and every power of evil, to make of our bodies and the world a new creation.

But more than this—here is a great mystery!—it is crucified human and divine weakness that made the universe from nothing *in the beginning*. Remember Athanasius: It is precisely the crucified, wounded Savior who is the Creator of the world (*Contra Gentes* 2.2).

We might take that praise in a weak sense, assuming Athanasius means only that Jesus first creates and later saves the world he has made. That cannot be what is meant, however, because creation is not an event within time, the most distant point of the past. We need instead to take what Athanasius says in a strong sense, even if that proves impossible for us to theorize: The cross is at the very root of all things that exist.

Because of who and *whose* Jesus is—the Son of the Father—Jesus's passion is not one event among many but the reality that determines the shape and direction and outcome of *all realities*. John Behr puts it this way:

> Creation and its history begins with the Passion of Christ and from this "once for all" work looks backwards and forwards to see everything in this light, making everything new. Christian cosmology, elaborated as it must be from the perspective of the Cross, sees the Cross as impregnated in the very structure of creation: *stat crux dum volvitur orbis*—the Cross stands, while the earth revolves. The power of God revealed in and through the Cross brought creation into being and sustains it in existence.[1]

Because of who and *whose* he is—the Son of the Father, the Lamb slain before the foundation of the world—Jesus never stands outside our situation as a casual observer. Jesus knows our excruciating plight as persons bound to die. God knows this in the person of the Son from the inside.

A poem of the last century, "Jesus of the Scars," tries to approach the mystery of the mystery: "The other gods were strong; but thou wast weak / They rode, but thou didst stumble to a throne / But to our wounds only God's wounds can speak / And not a god has wounds, but thou alone."[2] John Stott says it this way:

> In the real world of pain, how could one worship a God who was immune to it? I have entered many Buddhist temples in different Asian countries and stood respectfully before the statue of the Buddha, his legs crossed, arms folded, eyes closed, the ghost of a smile playing round his mouth, a remote look on his face,

> detached from the agonies of the world. But each time after a while I have had to turn away. And in imagination I have turned instead to that lonely, twisted, tortured figure on the cross, nails through hands and feet, back lacerated, limbs wrenched, brow bleeding from thorn-pricks, mouth dry and intolerably thirsty, plunged in godforsaken darkness. . . . "The cross of Christ . . . is God's only self-justification in such a world" as ours.[3]

When Jesus gives his back to *our* beating, and his hands and feet to *our* nails, when he allows us to murder *him*, this profound self-giving is not merely a *reflection* of the love of the Father. Jesus the Son says only what he hears his Father saying and does only what he sees his Father doing. And what his face shows us is the face of the Father. Jesus is the face of divine and human union.

In a great mystery, God was *in* Christ Jesus, reconciling the world to himself. This is a reckless, immoderate, unrestrained charity.

Some late-arriving teachers talk about the cross as a sacrifice that appeases the Father so that he can be reconnected with humanity. Sometimes this teaching goes so far as to suggest that the Father cannot even look at us, must keep his gaze on Jesus.

But this badly misses that Jesus and the Father are one, forgets the words of Jesus to Philip, "Whoever has seen me has seen the Father" (John 14:9). God has already drawn as close to humans as possible—and even closer!—in Jesus Christ, and in this Son he is looking upon sinners, touching sinners, dining with sinners, talking with sinners, suffering with sinners, healing and forgiving sinners *before* dying for all humans.

If God cannot look upon sinners, cannot come in contact with sinners, cannot inhabit the same space as sinners, then Jesus is not God and God is not like Jesus. No one describes the radical identification of God with humanity like the German martyr Dietrich Bonhoeffer: "God loves human beings. God loves the world. Not an ideal human, but human beings as they are; not an ideal world, but the real world. . . . What we shrink back from with pain and hostility, namely, real human beings, the real world, that is for God the ground of unfathomable love."[4]

The Father sows the Son along the path, between the rocks, among the thorns, and upon the good earth. He scatters the lowliness and gentleness they together are into the field that is the world. The Father lets the Son fall indiscriminately from his hand on us all, into every circumstance we humans are born into or inflict on ourselves and others. The Son's life is buried in trust with ours as one of us, as all of us.

The Father causes this Seed to mature *through* (strangely, not despite) all the brutal consequences of our sins and by water and the Spirit always brings to fruition the beautiful, fragrant harvest of all bodies along with the Son in the resurrection and ascension: "So shall my [Word] be that goes out from my mouth; it shall not return to me empty, but it shall accomplish that which I purpose and succeed in the thing for which I sent it" (Isa. 55:11).

One can be excused for getting the idea from some teachers that humans need to be saved from God, from their own Father, their own Maker. The first Christians were a lot clearer: Humans need rescue from the enemy of all humans, death. We need saving from the horrific wage sin imposed on us all and on the creation when we walked away from Love.

It must be self-evident that humanity needs rescue from sin, violence, and death. A God who participates in sin, violence, and death—a Father we cannot trust—is not other than fallen humanity but a projection of our worst fears and hatreds. A God who liberates us from sin, violence, and death—a Father we can trust—is good and welcome news from outside ordinary human experience and thought.

Brian Zahnd wisely preaches the union of the Father and the Son at the cross: "The cross is not where Jesus saves us from God, but where Jesus reveals God as savior. The cross is not what God inflicts upon Jesus in order to forgive, but what God in Christ endures as he forgives. . . . The cross is where the world violently sinned its sins in the body of the Son of God, and where he absorbed it all, praying, 'Father, forgive them!'"[5]

The world of suffering we cause and go on causing ought to overwhelm our senses and rend our hearts. Our lack of humility has made the work of God arduous, and God in the human flesh of Jesus works hard to redeem us.

We can make so much of the infinite strength of God that we lose sight that in the Son's humanity our evil caused God great travail. There was nothing easy about the cross for Jesus, and there should be nothing about the cross that does not disturb us.

Mercifully, most of us have never had to page through a file of horrific crime scene photos, but if we had the photos of the body of Jesus—the body of God—his bloody corpse would sicken and haunt us.

What have we done?

It ought to be hard for us to understand the cross. It ought to be difficult to contemplate our slaying of God. As terrifying as it must have been to witness it, pondering its meaning at our depths should not be less overwhelming, for the cross is *our* murder and rejection of the divine Love that is embodied in Jesus Christ. The cross is *our* murder and rejection of the new humanity of which Jesus Christ is the firstfruits. We should never be afraid of God; we should be afraid of ourselves. Herbert McCabe tells us why:

> The fact that to be human means to be crucified is not something that the Father has directly planned but what we have arranged. We have made a world in which there is no way of being human

> that does not involve suffering. . . . So my thesis is that Jesus died of being human. His very humanity meant that he put up no barriers, no defenses against those he loved who hated him. He refused to evade the consequences of being human in our inhuman world. So the cross shows up our world for what it really is, what we have made it. It is a world in which it is dangerous, even fatal, to be human; a world structured by violence and fear.[6]

On this, the first apostolic preachers in Acts are unanimous: *You killed Jesus.* God has nothing whatsoever to do with the crime. And the killing of Christ is what we go on doing. Over and over and over again, we live by the creed that someone else must be killed to make the world right.

This is what the terrorist believes. This is what the executioner believes when our societies sentence criminals to death and kill them. This is what the father who does not want to keep his unborn child believes: Someone else must die for the world to be made well. And that is the voice of satan.

What the execution of the Son of God means, if it means anything, is that no one else has to be killed in order for the world to be made right again. Not one more person has to die to balance a scale, to ensure that we have enough of whatever it is, to satisfy vengeance, to make my life more convenient, to improve the quality of another person's existence—add any deadly rationale that comes to mind.

Chris Green wants to reorient this bloodthirstiness in us by helping us sit before the cross, mindful of the character of God, for part of what afflicts us is amnesia about the image in which we are molded: "Golgotha is neither an act of God against us nor an act of God against God for us. It is the act of God with God with us against death and all deathly powers. It is a sacrifice, yes; but what makes it what it is, is that it is a sacrifice in which 'the living remains alive'—*in death*, and 'after' it."[7]

"[Jesus Christ] is 'the perfect sacrifice' primarily, if not exclusively, in the sense that he saves us from imagining God needs or wants the shedding of blood."[8] Christ the angel stays the hand of Abraham to show us that sacrifice is not what this God requires. Though all the ancient "gods" crave blood, David and the prophets understood that this God *does not*, as they try so very hard to tell us.

This God requires not sacrifice but a contrite heart in which the highways to the holy mountain can be traced, highways God reconstructs in our core by the Spirit, reconnecting us to the divine blueprint in which our hearts were made.

This God *provides* the sacrifice in himself. Again, Green observes, "[Christ's] offering of himself not only redeemed Cain's sacrifice but also raised Abel from the dead and reconciled him to his brother."[9]

What makes following Jesus so very different from everyday experience, from our ordinary attraction and addiction to power, is that the authentic Christ follower refuses to enact the sentence, "You must die so that I can exist" but rather gambles everything on the truth of the sentence, "Even if I die, the world God wants can and will exist." Stanley Hauerwas says that if in a hundred years Christians are known as the people who refuse to kill their children and their elderly, we will have done well.[10]

We will all die, and many more will be slain because we forget who we are, but Christians—as people who believe that the death of Christ is the only death that can make the world right again, who trust that when as a human God dies for the world he loves that death itself dies—ought to be the people who say to the spirit of Cain in all the ways that spirit arises in us, "No more!"

The crucifixion becomes the cross at the intersection of what we do to God by violence and what God does for us by love.

The beautiful God turns what humans intend for evil into good, turns the crowd's "His blood be on us and on our children" (Matt. 27:25) into an unwitting prayer, turns their curse into a blessing, for his blood saves wherever it lands. God takes the curse right out of our mouths and makes our treacherous breath an infinite blessing.

When Jesus prays *to* the Father to forgive his torturers, he is singing the forgiving heart of his Father back to him. When Jesus prays *with* the Father, even at the desperate margins of his tortured humanity, as life slips from his body, he is singing the forgiveness that they simply are together as one God with their Spirit, the song they forever sing and which they want us to sing.

And there is another beautiful mystery at work here: Jesus, as the one sinless human, the only One who has become truly human and is worthy to pray these words on humanity's behalf as one of us within the divine life, prays that prayer as one of us, for us. And he prays it over those who torture and kill him.

What wondrous love is this? Those who crucify—those who bring terror—are as forgiven and held by God in Jesus Christ as those who bear the brunt of terror, as those who are crucified. Not to ratify anyone's evil but to draw evil out of us. We are kidding ourselves if we think we can get our heads around *that* kind of charity.

We can try to articulate a facet of this mystery, following Dostoevsky and Bonhoeffer, by speaking the gospel: The human God is a judge who puts himself in the soiled, broken shoes of the accused, desires to be numbered among the guilty, takes responsibility for all of us, and it's in part this radical solidarity that makes the healing God brings actual, restorative, and inclusive.

Every human—each of us a mixture of the oppressor and the oppressed—stands under the inexplicable hardwood pardon of the cross.

This is deep Christianity: Following Jesus, the human who takes responsibility for all of us, a Christian can never really insulate themselves from the sin of anyone else.

Here we draw the sharpest contrast between our current culture and the culture the cross is trying to bring: When it comes to victim statements at the sentencing phase of our trials, it is often clear that no one involved in trying a criminal and no one in the community feels they have anything at all to do with the convict. All onus falls on the perpetrator, who is dehumanized, and any suggestion that responsibility (not guilt) belongs anywhere else is almost unthinkable. We need the human God to help us see ourselves in everyone who stands accused, for it is this imagination that makes authentic mercy even thinkable, much less doable. This imagination helps us to name in ourselves what led to their actions and helps us resist othering them.

Every human—each of us a mixture of the oppressor and the oppressed—stands under the inexplicable hardwood pardon of the cross.

Without erasing any evidence, God brings the deepest healing to the evil we do (and to the evil that has been done to us), a healing that's beyond any possibility we can enforce or conjure because God includes all those who do harm (us also) in the sort of restoration and wholeness he brings.

The best our systems can do is bring proximate justice. But, if we are honest, even the proximate justice we bring is often complicated by its own evil. It can do nothing to restore what's been lost—a person, for instance—or make a world where any harm is no longer capable of happening.

When in the end God's healing extends to the cosmos, *all potential causes of harm* and *all actual harms* will be burned out of the fallen order of things by the fire of Love.

In the church, we don't use the word *mystery* to describe something we don't know anything about. When we are encountered by a mystery, we know something has happened, yet every time we draw close to the event—every time we think we know what it's about and have seen it whole—its meaning is revealed as deeper and larger than we thought. Its full measure escapes us. The cross transcends our every description, including this attempt.

But we will try, once again, to ponder the cross with Sharad Yadav:

> Nothing captures the reality of the world's pain and sorrow more than the story of God (the single, ineffable, utterly unknown ground of all there is) making himself personally known in the suffering of a marginalized, poor, brown-skinned peasant in the most inconsequential ghetto of the most powerful empire on earth, living in a love so profound that it threatened the most elite institutional . . . guardians of reality, causing them to conspire to murder him. To me, that nakedness, vulnerability, forgiveness, and self-giving is God, and the resurrection simply means that this love can't be killed. . . . Either that or he isn't, it won't, and all competing claims of ultimacy in life are just other faces for the same powers that killed him.[11]

And yet we are the humans who trust for all humans that God "canceled the record of the charges against us and took it away by nailing it to the cross" (Col. 2:14 NLT) and that by the cross Christ "stripped all the spiritual tyrants in the universe of their sham authority" and "marched them naked through the streets" (2:15 Message).

And the cross is ten thousand things besides, but let us try, yet one more time, to speak wisely of the cross: To become human is to die for the life of the world and to be raised to life without end within it beyond death. There is only one human who is human in this way. His life is now our life, his death is now our death, his story is now our story, and the end of his story is the only good ending to the human story, a story we can begin living now by the Spirit.

In the summer of 2014, as ISIS lay siege to Syria and northern Iraq, more than a thousand Chaldean Catholics gathered in Hart Plaza in downtown Detroit to pray and protest. I stood in the circle they formed, most carrying blood-red crosses of various sizes and wearing blood-red ribbons in solidarity with their friends and loved ones.

Bishop Francis Kalabat told us that many Iraqi Christians were asking him, "Where is God while our sisters and brothers, our parents and children are being maimed and killed?" He stopped, and pointing to a large red crucifix on the lawn behind him, the bloodied body of Jesus hanging from it, he said, "*That* is where our God is! Jesus *suffers* and is in this suffering *with us*."

That kind of love inspires repentance. That kind of love inspires us to love everyone. That kind of love inspires us to be human as God is human in Jesus Christ, and that means taking up our cross and following him.

We take up our cross by living in the world as the human God lives (someone who is patient and kind; someone who does not insist on his own way; someone who bears, believes, hopes, and endures all things). We take up our cross by standing in the world where the human God stands (not rejoicing in the wrong but rejoicing in the right). We take up our cross by speaking in the world as the human God speaks (not arrogant, boastful, rude, jealous, irritable, or resentful). We take up our cross by following the personification of Love. That personification has a name, and it's the sweetest name we know.

DEAD

Every human hopes to be remembered, even the human who is God.

On the evening before he dies, at a meal with his friends—though they think of themselves as something less than that—Jesus says, "Remember me."

It is a hard truth of existence that eventually the living will forget all but a few of those who have died. And those who are remembered are rarely remembered truly. Time wipes our fingerprints from the surfaces we have touched, scatters our ashes in wind and water, forgets our having been here. As soon as our family and close friends and acquaintances are also dead and gone, there is for most of us no living human memory of us.

Somewhere deep down we know we are not made to be forgotten. There is something about us that requires everlastingness. This is the contradiction Ecclesiastes names for us: Eternity has been set in our hearts, yet our lives are vapor.

God asks to be remembered! Christ entrusts us with his remembrance. Why, given that our lives are so narrow and brief and our memories so faulty? What can the infinite ask of the finite?

Those of us called to this work of remembering are often the first to forget. We forget that God, by God's own decision, is known forever by the words, will, creativity, mind, tears, joys, actions—and, yes, frailty—of a particular human being.

We forget that what it means to be God is forever bound to this human the angel tells Mary and Joseph to name Jesus and that what it means to be human is forever bound to the God Jesus calls Abba.

If we do not remember the human who tells us to put away our swords and to love our enemies, if we do not remember that he forgives us even as we torture and murder him, we have forgotten God and forgotten that God is human. If we do not visit the sick or the prisoner, if we do not welcome the immigrant, if we do not feed the hungry and give water to the thirsty, we have forgotten God and forgotten that God is human.

To remember Jesus is to know God and to make God known so that our neighbors can know the love in which they live and move and have their being—the love that shows itself in the way Jesus lived and in the way he died.

Make no mistake, to remember Jesus as the God who suffers with us is to hear a call to be present where he is—in the embrace of the Father and *among the suffering*. To remember that God suffers with us in Christ is to know our sufferings do not define us or determine our fate.

Jesus is the living human who remembers what it is like to be a dead man.

Jesus is the living human who remembers what it is like to be a dead man. He remembers us too, and it is right not only to give him thanks and praise but also to remind him that we whom he remembers, whom he lived among and died with and for, are still dying, lying in the streets of the northern suburbs of Kiev and the southern kibbutzim of Israel, buried beneath the fallen apartment buildings of Mariupol, Aleppo, and Gaza City, slain in the villages of the Sudan and the Congo and gunned down in the squares of Iran, blown to kingdom come in churches and train stations and hospitals.

It is righteous to ask with the psalmist "How long?" as we weep with the human God who with us sees his brothers' and sisters' bodies turned to ash and stone by death and to cry out, "Wake up, dead man! Arise and restore us to life!"

In my work as a chaplain for first responders, I see a lot of death up close. I see its effects on bodies and on loved ones: suicides of young and old persons, accidental and unexpected deaths of children, premeditated murders, the horrific aftermath of the Oxford High School shooting just after Thanksgiving 2021.

I have seen that the dying have many faces and understand something of why Paul was moved to name death the last enemy (1 Cor. 15:26).

Death is not God's doing. The Wisdom of Solomon says it more clearly and directly than any other part of Scripture:

> God did not make death,
> and he does not delight in the destruction of the living.
> For he created all things so that they might exist; . . .
> God created us for incorruption,
> and made us in the image of his own eternity,
> but through an adversary's envy death entered the world.
> (1:13–14; 2:23–24)

David Bentley Hart read about a man who lost his children to the Boxing Day tsunami in 2004 and imagines how awful it would be for someone to tell that man God had taken his children because of some eternal logic or divine plan. Hart says such words would offer no "credible comfort," not only because they are in the moment cruel and unwise but also because they "deny that man a knowledge central to the gospel: the knowledge of the evil of death, its intrinsic falsity, its unjust dominion over the world, its ultimate nullity; the knowledge that God is not pleased or nourished by our deaths, that he is not the secret architect of evil, that he is the conqueror of hell, that he has condemned all these things by the power of the cross; the knowledge that God is life and light and infinite love."[1]

Hart calls for an entirely different response, one that emphasizes God's compassion for the bereaved: "As for comfort, when we seek it, I can imagine none greater than the happy knowledge that when I see the death of a child, I do not see the face of God but the face of his enemy."[2]

Death is a great complexity, and our theologies of death must resist simplicities and platitudes. Death is not always accidental or sudden; it does not always bring about great tragedy or leave loved ones in desperate straits. It sometimes comes as rest and at least appears peaceful. Some live to a very old age or suffer for a long time so that their death comes finally as a comfort or as relief from great or long-standing pain.

Still, even the death of someone who has "completed" their life is a great loss to those who love them and to the world, a rending if not a violent rupture, a tear in space-time, for a world dies with every human who dies, and the cosmos dies a bit also.

It is important to start out all our conversations about death with the ancient wisdom that God desires the death of no one, that God opposes the sin and envy that have brought death into the world, that Christ has, in the words of the Easter liturgy, "tramp[led] down death by death."[3]

Death is no longer death, thanks to Jesus, even though we continue to experience it as rupture and violation. Rather than clinging to life, afraid of death, we can voluntarily lay down our lives, as Christ did, giving ourselves up for the life of the world. John Behr explains:

> Through his Passion, destroying death by death, Christ has enabled us to *use* our death, the fact of our mortality, *actively*. Rather than being passive and frustrated victims of the givenness of our mortality, complaining that it is not fair, or doing all we can to secure ourselves, we now have a path open to us, through a voluntary death in baptism, to enter the body and life of Christ. . . . In doing this, our new existence is grounded in the free self-sacrificial love that Christ has shown to be the life and very being of God himself, for as we have seen Christ has shown us what it is to be God in the way he dies as a human being.[4]

By showing us what it is to be God by the way he dies, Jesus has made death a wholly owned subsidiary of the kingdom of heaven. In the death he dies for us, the eternal Son transfigures death into a doorway to life. Because the Lord converts death to life and breath to spirit, there can now be something called a good death, something that makes our dead bodies a sign of something good already coming into the world, the assurance of the restoration of all things.

BURIED

These days we rarely see death up close. A hundred years ago, at least one sibling would die in childhood, and parents often died before they saw their grandchildren.

When we do die, we too often die alone in nursing homes or hospitals. I know, because I am called to attend these deaths when no one comes.

In older times, you died at home, surrounded by your family, who washed your body after you died and dressed your body for burial, then put you on ice while neighbors and friends came by the house to visit for a day or two. They then dug your grave themselves and lowered you into the ground, sending you into the dark with prayers and songs and tears.

Now the body is taken away immediately, handled by strangers, paid to do work we do not want to do ourselves, and the body is often cremated. Other strangers dig the graves. Often, the body is not present at whatever memorial service occurs, whether in a church or in a funeral home, and sometimes these services occur months after the day of death.

There is psychological, physical, and spiritual health in the work of washing bodies, building caskets, and digging graves. Not everyone can or will do these things, and one understands how it can be a relief to have others do them, but it is vital to be there for someone's last words and final breath. We need to witness the bodies of loved ones lowered six feet under (even our small children need to witness this).

Our bodies are deeply important and inseparable from us because God has a body exactly like ours, a body that died, a body that had to be prepared for burial, a body that was entombed, a body that mourners attended to, wept over, and laid in the ground with their own hands and hearts. In the end, before they turned away, they might have kissed his shrouded forehead.

My friend Paddy Lynch, a mortician, has taught me a lot about dead bodies. He says that they are, like newborn babies, the most vulnerable of humans and that what we do for the dead in their death is the highest form of mercy we can perform.

Why? Because the dead cannot do anything for us. Even more than newborns, they are beyond returning the mercy we give them in cherishing their bodies and laying them to rest.

At Lynch & Sons, they treat dead bodies with tremendous dignity. Paddy's uncle, Thomas Lynch, says it this way: "The bodies of the newly dead are not debris nor remnant, nor are they entirely icon or essence. They are, rather, changelings, incubates, hatchlings of a new reality that bear our names and dates, our image and likenesses, as surely in the eyes and ears of our children and grandchildren as did word of our birth in the ears of our parents and their parents. It is wise to treat such *new* things tenderly, carefully, with honor."[1]

Paddy says that dead bodies are a sign to us of the resurrection. As one Scottish undertaker told Eric Peterson, a cemetery is holy ground, a plot of earth that belongs to God—"God's acre," he called it—and "within it are buried the seeds of resurrection."[2] The death of Christ has carved a furrow into existence, a furrow into which we are planted in our dying by the Spirit as seeds of a new creation.

In this sense, all cemeteries, all burial grounds, all mausoleums—everywhere that a human has been buried, everywhere their ashes are scattered—are the places in the world from which a renewal of the whole cosmos will spring. But first we must die and first we must be laid in the ground.

Johannes Baptist Metz says that "Satan wants to make Jesus strong, for what the devil really fears is the powerlessness of God in the humanity Christ has assumed."[3] If what Metz says is true, then the dead body of Jesus, lying still in the cool shadows of the grave, is the undoing of the devil and the end of death, however hard that is to imagine or trust.

Jesus died, let himself be dead and buried, became as dead as a doornail, to arrest our descent into nonexistence by placing himself beneath all things. Now, no matter how far humanity falls, no matter how far any single person falls, we land on the dead body of Jesus, who died to make himself and his experience the limit of our descent.

Christians trust this mystery: God is dead—really dead—and those who like Peter have gotten behind Christ, those who follow him on the road that leads to Golgotha and beyond it, join him in his death through the sacrament of baptism and by mystical participation in his sufferings.

We did our worst to him—remember, he is in the tomb "so disfigured he seemed hardly human" (Isa. 52:14 NET)—and yet we could not keep him from being God for us. Even dead, he remains the Lord. For him, dying is not at odds with what it means to be God but somehow a startling revelation of what it means to be God from eternity.

The mystery of the human God is great: The true giver of life, who gives life to all things, who alone loves all the things he makes, accepts the condition of actual death in order that all things might have his kind of life.

Israel's priests were prohibited from handling corpses, yet Jesus not just handles the dead but becomes a dead corpse—one among the discarded dead bodies. This dead body is God's. This dead body is what it means to be the Creator and the One who in patience and humility serves in love what he creates. As one of the ancient Christian theologians, Gregory Nazianzen, says, "We needed a God made flesh and made dead, that we might live."[4]

Robert Farrar Capon writes:

> [Christ] doesn't just take a three-day nap in the tomb and then come blithely out, ignoring the subject of death like some transmigration-of-souls guru. By the fact that he's God, he has those three dead days eternally present in himself. And when he comes to us in our deaths, he brings us into his death before he lifts us into his resurrection. As his death is the historical sacrament, the real presence, of the new creation, so our death is our personal sacrament of that same reconciled order. It's something we're supposed to celebrate, not take the edge off with pipe dreams of immortality. Death is the choicest piece of evidence we have for our resurrection.[5]

If the body of Jesus remains the body of God in his death, we should resist saying that the dead body of any human is not that person anymore, for what is true of the human God is true of all humans.

Have you seen Hans Holbein's *Dead Christ*? If you stare at it long enough, a great hope takes hold. If you remain with Jesus in his death long enough, you begin to understand that stillness and weakness are the very conditions from which God makes all things new. Here in the tomb of our shattered existence, the wounded God puts his arms around us and invites us to trust in his wounds; here the Spirit draws us into the wounds of the human God.

Jesus invites us to trust his wounds and his death, because the gospel is not first the news that we can receive Jesus into our lives; the gospel is first and foremost that Jesus has received us into his death. When we at last are dead, God is finally able to do something with us, can finally redeem everything about us—precisely because we can do nothing to resist his saving work. All things must pass from death to life through his person, the One in whom nothing divine is absent, nothing human lacking. Ponder these things as if the death of Jesus is your death because it is—and because his life is now your life.

When we encounter Jesus Christ, we don't live to tell about it. We die with him, showing that by the weakness of his cross (and ours) joy has entered the world. There is nothing more life-giving or converting or transfiguring than to at long last fall into the arms of God crucified and buried. His dead body is so life-giving, so creative, so re-creative.

There is nothing more life-giving or converting or transfiguring than to at long last fall into the arms of God crucified and buried.

The body of Jesus is buried in the earth, the soil from which all earthenware creatures come and to which all return. Christ descends to the center of our longsuffering earth as earth that suffers. And as Christ rises from the ground, he does not leave earth behind, but in his risen body brings the earth with him into the glory of God, the firstfruits of Mother Earth's eventual and total healing.

From his stillness in the grave, from what looks like the end of all things, a new creation springs to life in us and in the world. Pascha—the whole movement from cross to burial to descent to resurrection to ascension—is the "big bang" that in the beginning makes everything from nothing, eternity working "backward" from the event. It is this "big bang" that in the end makes Christ all in all, eternity working "forward" from the event.

Peter tells us that after his death Jesus goes and preaches to the spirits in prison (1 Pet. 3:19). And what does this preacher preach?

This is what he preaches: The time is here. The kingdom has arrived. Repent. Believe this gospel (even if it all seems too good to be true) because it is trustworthy. We can venture everything on Jesus Christ, our human brother, with us in all our prisons and our hells.

Our Maker made like us, made one of us, is the high priest who hears the truth in our tears of shattered anguish, who discerns the goodness in our laughs of purest joy, who delights in them with us just as he delights with us in the sound of the wind in the trees and of birdsong. He knows better than we can the dread of our courtrooms and the silence of our cemeteries. He knows what it is to be godforsaken. He has made his bed in hell.

As elder Sophrony teaches us, "Be sure that as long as there is someone in hell, Christ will be there with them."[6] He who traversed the great chasm of death by his cross still sits in hell with every "rich man." He will never stop loving him, will never stop working to make his heart capable of seeing the invisible realities that are the beginning of contentment.

The great medieval seer Julian of Norwich sees this and more: "Adam fell from life to death, into the valley of this wretched world, and after that into hell. God's Son fell with Adam, into the valley of the womb of the maiden, who was the fairest daughter of Adam, and that was to excuse Adam from blame in heaven and on earth; and powerfully he brought him out of hell."[7]

With his nail-scarred hands on our shoulders, Jesus makes us a promise: "Do not be afraid; I am the First and the Last and the

Living One. I was dead, and see, I am alive forever and ever, and I have the keys of Death and of Hades" (Rev. 1:17–18).

If you find yourself in hell, a victim of natural disaster, drowned by your own ruined heart and participations in evil—do not be afraid or lose hope. A preacher is going to come, the crucified Creator, who is endlessly patient, who loves you. This preacher remembers mercy and blots out your sins.

When we pray, we pray to this preacher: the One who rules all times and places, who made all things seen and unseen, now made judge of his human brothers and sisters by the things he suffered, and his judgment ends in this command: "Come forth!" (John 11:43 KJV).

Because of our brother's death we all have a future, a future that is present and available in every moment of time, a future that heals everything and everyone, a future we call resurrection.

A HUMAN FUTURE

Without the resurrection there might be a spiritual world and a life after death, but that also might be no better than this world in which we live with its poverty, hatred, power-driven egotism, misery, war, brutality, systematized torture, . . . pain, agony and despair. A spiritual dimension without the resurrection might well be far worse than extinction.

—Morton Kelsey, *Resurrection*

Only *love* can believe the resurrection.

—Ludwig Wittgenstein,
Culture and Value

Jesus . . . speaks to God his Father in a human voice. In heaven, the language they speak is human, not just angelic.

—Rowan Williams, homily for Feast of the Ascension,
May 21, 2009

The life of the church, lived in solidarity with those in darkness, carries with it the embodiment of a certainty: when he comes again, it will be the God of mercy and no one else, and it will be morning.

—Fleming Rutledge, *Advent*

MARY

A new creation starts at the moment of Jesus's death. There is an earthquake, and the veil of the temple is torn from top to bottom, and "the saints," their bones reduced to ashes by the slow grind of time, emerge from their graves (Matt. 27:51–52).

We are told by Matthew that the tombs of many of the dead are opened, that their *bodies* are raised from their tombs, and that they are seen "walking around the holy city" (Matt. 27:53). These are not the "walking dead" of our contemporary cinema but humans somehow made actually, beautifully alive. They are now the truly living. Matthew reports that all of this happens in the moment that Jesus breathes his last, as he pours out his Spirit—three days before the resurrection. There's something about the death of Jesus, about the very moment of his death, as C. S. Lewis understood, that causes death to begin to work backward.[1]

The death of Jesus works its way back into the whole history of the house of Israel, and through Israel and the obedience of this one human, into all humanity.

His sacrifice for the sins of the whole world begins reversing death at Golgotha and there is no moment before or since in which resurrection is not at work like leaven in bread. Our God is not the God of the dead but the God of the living. In Christ no one who dies stays dead.

Early on Easter morning, we find Mary Magdalene heartbroken because the body she prepared with love for burial has vanished, the face and the voice that called her back to herself are gone (John 20:11–18).

Here in the rising light, in the garden, there is—as at the grave of Lazarus—a tomb and a stone and more grave clothes, and more tears. Then at her lowest point, and at the world's seeming end, Mary hears the voice of her rabbi, the same voice that called Lazarus forth, and turns to see his risen face.

Unlike her mother Eve, Mary encounters not the snake but the Gardener, not the voice of deception but embodied truth, not the slithering destroyer who kills but the One who in the beginning breathed all things into existence.

If Mary Magdalene is in John's account of the resurrection a new Eve, then Jesus is, of course, the new Adam. Mary mistakes him for the gardener. Could it be that when she encounters him, he has his hands in the soil, as he so often does, caring for and healing the creation, perhaps planting chrysanthemums?

The scars on the mud-covered palms of Jesus tell the difficult, glorious story: Jesus, the man from Nazareth, born under a cloud of rumors to the woman everyone knows was unmarried when she conceived him—this One who used to get sawdust in his hair making tables with Joseph—is now forever the God with wounds, not resuscitated but somehow raised to a new kind of never-ending embodied life.

And, yes, you have to have a body to bear the marks of slaughter.

How extraordinary: Mary mistakes Jesus for the gardener. Apparently, you can miss Christ's magnificence because his posture is so down-to-earth, his bearing is so humble. He's not floating three inches above the grass; he's not glowing with ghostly energy; he's not distant or detached or disinterested in the world. God looks at home in the garden. God looks like he works the soil (because he does). God looks like a servant (because he is).

Any story that makes you devalue this world—that makes you scoff at mud and flowers and sunrises and gardening, at welcoming the people some despise or ignore, at knowing and calling them by name—has nothing to do with resurrection.

Resurrection means getting back to gardening as the primary vocation of humanity. Resurrection means welcoming the anonymous stranger and hearing their good news. Resurrection means getting back to cooking, hosting, and celebrating as the primary form of human recreation. Resurrection means trusting what you haven't seen for yourself. Resurrection means that this world God made matters. Resurrection means that the race of humans matters to God. After all, God is one of us and one with us.

When we first encounter her in this story, Mary Magdalene is crying. I imagine her collapsed on the ground in sorrow, lost because her beloved is dead, in shock because even his body is now gone. Then Jesus her teacher speaks her name, and perhaps it is the way he says her name that turns her around in astonishment.

The world still lives with Mary's tears. The world has yet to recognize the Master in the guise of the gardener. And the world is still chaotic and dark and untrustworthy.

There is the little girl who accidentally gets run over in the driveway.

There are dozens killed by a missile while they are worshiping. I try to imagine what it must be like for my brothers and sisters when murder and hatred show up in their sacred space as they worship our Lord. I try to imagine those last moments of terror before the end.

The world still lives with Mary's tears. The world has yet to recognize the Master in the guise of the gardener.

There's the mother of young children who's told her battle with cancer is ending, that the thief we call cancer is taking her away from them.

So many of us have lost—or are losing—so many dear ones. We can multiply true stories of unimaginable sorrow.

When we live in denial of real-life struggles (and denial can be simply tuning out the shadows with false enthusiasm), it's hard for the world to receive our very good news that all this death is not the end, that the death of Jesus means that death is now everywhere in retreat, even if we cannot usually see that.

It is also harder for us to engage suffering strangers and acquaintances with authentic compassion, mercy, and empathy when we refuse to stay with Jesus at the crosses or tombs of life or forget that that is where he always is until the end of time.

It is hard to be patient in our own sufferings or endure the anguish of those closest to us—to see our troubles as a participation in Christ's hardships—when we expect every day to be Easter.

When we live in denial, it is hard to sustain honest community, to engender churches where folks who doubt and struggle with faith and obedience are as welcome as those who are certain and assured.

And so, we stay with Mary's tears. We ponder the pall that has been cast over the whole creation. We ponder every vigil, every wake, every funeral, every unexpected, sudden goodbye.

We ponder billions who lived and then were gone, often with no record of having ever been here, and with them the whole world that is lost inside every person any time any human dies, and the loss their absence is for the world.

Yet in this time, as we endure our personal and corporate seasons of trial and trauma, dying and burying, in this time before Christ's kingdom comes here on earth as it is in heaven, we do not wait as those without hope. Hope keeps us in the waiting room without despair.

We wait in a tension between the gloom of Holy Saturday, when the still-dead body of Jesus lies like a stone in the grave, and the bright promise of Easter. Some days we have faith, and on other days we must rely on the faith of others. Thanks be to God we are not saved alone but accompanied in this journey by the body of Christ—and the prayers of Jesus that are the soul of that body.

And as we face down death together, we have a message to deliver. But before we do that, we must leave the garden.

Mary wants to stay with Jesus—who can blame her?—but the gospel is not lived in the garden. The gospel is lived in a Good Friday world. The gospel is lived in the shadows that look and feel a lot like Holy Saturday, when God seems absent. The gospel is lived on the Monday *after* Easter, as the bright colors, hymns, and feast fade, as life stays busy, expensive, even dangerous, as the world remains tragicomic.

Jesus "goes away" and sends Mary away too because resurrection belongs outside the garden, in the world of car bombings and sexual abuse and petty theft, in the world where principalities seek to separate everyone from everyone.

Resurrection belongs in the basement with a family grieving the death of their young daughter by her own hand. They need reminders of the resurrection. Resurrection needs legs and hands and hearts and voices of witness.

We are Jesus's witnesses that he is indeed alive. And we must depart the garden and go where he is calling us to bring the new creation, to breathe out into his good world the news of the resurrection, to be by our lives the fragrance of the resurrection, to forgive all by the resurrection. And we all follow Mary Magdalene, who was the first of us humans to announce this gospel.

RESURRECTION

It is not the memory of Jesus that is enthroned in heaven but the eternal and human person we encounter in the Gospels. As Thomas Lynch, the mortician-essayist, reminds us, God raised not "the Idea of Jesus" from the tomb but his body.[1]

Jesus does not "live on" in the disciples' fondest wishes or projections or in the collective sentiments of everyone down the centuries who have trusted this story. Jesus lives on at the right hand of the Father, with scars until no one can be scarred again. John Henry Newman writes, "Philosophers of old time thought the soul indeed might live forever, but that the body perished at death; but Christ tells us otherwise, he tells us the body will live for ever."[2]

Humans are not ghosts in machines that somehow become disembodied spirits, nor are we mere material that dissipates into "oneness" with the rest of creation.

We are destined for an embodied existence in eternity. There, the things that make us who we are as one-of-a-kind divine image bearers—laughter, courage, generosity, brilliant thoughts and self-less deeds, skin and bones—will inhabit bodies that are transfigured in ways we do not as yet understand.

God keeps all the information (genetics) and all the mystery (the essence of every human soul) about us, and he knows how to raise us from death. That is real hope. That is real love. As Frederick Buechner confesses (with the church through the ages): Resurrection is not a "disembodied echo of a human being but a new and revised version of all the things that made [her] the particular [person she was] and which [she] needs something like a body to express: [her] personality, the way [she] looked, the sound of [her] voice, [her] peculiar capacity for creating and loving, in some sense [her] face."[3]

None of us have any idea how this "works" or precisely what it looks like, but we trust that this is somehow so.

Notice how John runs to the tomb of Jesus and how John immediately believes (John 20:3–9). There's something in the *way* the clothes are folded and set aside in the tomb. John sees in a moment that no one but a conscious and somehow embodied-after-death Jesus left the grave clothes in the exact way Jesus did, perhaps folded in a particular way taught by his temple seamstress mother. And John trusts.

We *oppose* the evil of death with all that we are in Christ, and we *embrace* the transfiguration of death with all that we are in Christ, who tells us that he is resurrection and life.

John tells us that "as yet they did not understand the scripture" that Jesus would rise from death (John 20:9), and yet John's love believes without seeing. Love believes all things (1 Cor. 13:7). Love trusts. Love hopes. When we trust someone we love, we believe in them.

God did not make death, and God has no partnership with it (Wis. of Sol. 1:13). God does not delight in the death of anyone (Ezek. 18:23). Death is the final enemy of God and the final enemy of man (1 Cor. 15:26), and we are permitted to hate it with perfect contempt. And yet death, having been trampled down by the death of the human God, has no sting now (15:55). Accepting our death is now the way to become human as God is human.

We *oppose* the evil of death with all that we are in Christ, and we *embrace* the transfiguration of death with all that we are in Christ, who tells us that he is resurrection and life, the One who has defeated death and the grave, who asks us, "Do you believe this?" And we are the ones who respond with Martha, "Yes, Lord, I believe that you are the Messiah, the Son of God, the one coming into the world" (John 11:27).

I had the privilege of sitting with a man about six years my junior, a man I had labored alongside for almost twenty years, a man who until his diagnosis with ALS had been the master of the young acolytes of our parish.

Scott Trautman was on the spectrum and one of the hardest-working humans I knew—clerking behind the counter at the local druggist, delivering for a bakery, serving the church. Everyone loved him.

It was hard to see him bedridden and on oxygen, the mask cutting furrows into his kind face. Eventually, he communicated via a computer that followed the movement of his eyes. It took time for his sentences to form, but when they were composed and sent, a digitized voice would read them to me.

It was a slow, contemplative way to converse. And what came through—in his tears, at the margins of his mouth, and via the spoken texts—was Scott's inexplicable courage to live at the intersection of fighting ALS with his entire self and a holy surrender to the inevitable. Scott's trust was both tough and tender. His room was a "thin place" between heaven and earth. Who, we might ask, was ministering to whom?

Scott held a bedrock trust in the communion of saints, in our union with those who in Christ are alive beyond death. This is something I, too, have learned to trust.

At a Eucharist in 1994 in San Antonio, I was standing at the back wall of a large sanctuary. Hundreds of people were coming forward to see and touch and taste God in bread and wine. Musicians were leading a song of praise; I raised my hands and sang. I had a palpable sense of the presence of my Pentecostal ancestors—my mother's father and my father's father on either side of me, their hands raised in song as they so often were in church—and I knew in my heart that they were truly there with us, were more truly present than any of us.

In one of our final moments together, Scott told me he knew that in dying he was becoming prayer and that he would in the resurrection intercede for his mother and me. *This* is what it means to join Martha's embodied trust in the resurrection—something unseen but more real than reality.

We are the ones who trust that the cosmos is ordered not to death or entropy but to resurrection because crucified love is stronger than death, that the weakness of God on the cross is stronger than any force of evil in the universe, that resurrection is more viral in the world than a pandemic, more contagious than any hatred.

On Holy Saturday in 2019, *The New York Times* published an interview with the president of Union Theological Seminary in which she mentioned a Christian "obsession" with the physicality of our Lord's resurrection.[4]

Count me among the obsessed.

There are many witnesses in the New Testament, but John's and Peter's testimonies that Jesus ate and drank with his disciples (John 21:15; Acts 10:41) and Luke's testimony that Jesus said, "A ghost does not have flesh and bones as you see that I have" (Luke

24:39) take the guesswork out of it for me, even if puzzlements remain. These texts describe someone who remains flesh of our flesh and bone of our bone *beyond* death.

Yes, the body of Jesus Christ walks through walls and vanishes and—before resurrection—walks on water. The body of Christ shows up differently: here in bread and wine, there in the poor and prisoner. There is great mystery here, no doubt, but we are talking about an *embodied mystery*. Not just skeptics and confused clergy have doubts. Resurrection is a great challenge to any of us who experience the real world.

Even so, Cyril of Alexandria reminds us, echoing Paul: If Jesus does not rise again in a body of flesh, indeed, in the very body he received from his mother and that was tortured and executed, and if he does not *remain* somehow embodied in eternity, then what sort of death is defeated? How can we trust that our own bodies will be made imperishable? There is no resurrection without a body, even if that body somehow transcends physics (*Commentary on the Gospel of John* 12.1).

Christ's resurrection (and by his ours) is not, as some have described it, mere "spiritual survival," a nonmaterial consolation for our lost bodies and a lost world. The first Christians are clear about this: The one human nature we all share has been rescued from death by the death and bodily resurrection of Jesus Christ, not just for a moment but forever.

We can struggle with the enormity of the resurrection and not comprehend it (who does?), and doubting is part of being human. Debating the mystery of it all is part of having faith in community with other persons. Yet resurrection is what we together trust.

Chris Green reminds us that it's always more than we can imagine: "[Christ's] resurrection is eschatological, not merely historical. It is not one more thing that happens to Jesus, but the happening of Jesus to all things. He is not changed; everything is changed."[5]

I stood by the casket of my father when I was four. I stood by the caskets of my sister and two of her children taken from us in an instant when their car overturned on a Utah highway. I've stood next to many humans in hospitals and on roadsides and in living rooms, some taken by violence, some taken by disease, some taken by time, and some taken by their own hand. I know how final it all seems.

I once heard a prominent American astrophysicist talk about observing dancers in a dimly lit ballroom. At old-school formals, the men wore black and the women wore white. Watching at a distance, you saw the women whirling about the room, held in the arms of their invisible partners.

The scientist was using this as an analogy for black holes. You know a black hole is there, he said, because you see the star circling it.

I trust Jesus's resurrection in the same way.

Not only because I see its effects in the lives of Jesus's disciples, but also because I can see grace encircling the lives of the people I care for as they die. I can see grace encircle even my life at times, in moments of inexplicable grief and pain as much as of joy and elation. And so I trust that resurrection is indeed there in the darkness.

Imagine that the person you most cherished in life, whom you never considered living without, whose absence makes you wonder whether you have ever lived as fully since their death or ever will again, shows up for dinner—not as a spirit but as the flesh-and-bones person whose loss you mourn. Your head struggles to catch up with what your heart is seeing and hearing and embracing. You experience a disbelieving joy as when something you thought forever lost is found, and your tears are the sign of a strange, inexplicable gladness you now grasp: Death is not the end of anyone; resurrection is.

What it means to suffer and die as a human is now transfigured by this person you see and hear and hold tight to your chest. None of their wounds are wasted. None of your wounds are wasted. You experience resurrection as your own destiny, your own end; this is what becomes of death: It dies. Meals and connection and conversation and laughter are what go on forever.

You're still a human facing death, so days (years) of fear, anxiety, peril, and sorrow are ahead, yet the courage to love your enemy is now rooted in a calm that is whispered into your deepest heart: "All things now participate in God's permanence."

And you do not trust the resurrection alone.

When in worship we say that we "remember the resurrection," we are joining the memory of these first witnesses, who saw Jesus alive and embodied beyond death, who are *at once* gathered with us and with God—that is, they are present at the end, at the resurrection of ourselves and all persons. In their experience, resurrection is *finished*.

George MacDonald, writing to his father in the spring of 1853 after the death of his brother, Alec, joins their vivid resurrection trust: "Of him we need never say he *was*; for what he was he is now—only expanded, enlarged and glorified. . . . Surely God that clothes the fields now with the wild flowers risen fresh from their winter graves, will keep Alec's beauty in His remembrance and not let a manifestation of Himself, as every human form is, so full of the true, simple, noble and pure, be forgotten."[6]

Everywhere Christ Jesus is (and there is nowhere he is not), he exhales a new creation, his divine and human breath making all things new. When we breathe the air of the resurrection, we forgive, and we remember the poor, and we love our enemies.

The resurrection is already at work in the world. And one day there will not be anywhere or (we hope and pray) anyone who is not transfigured by life without end.

Let me tell you something that happened to me once that helps me to trust in the resurrection.

It begins outside in the darkness. Scores of us gathered around the clergy and a choir of acolytes and many more in brown robes, like old-school friars' habits, some with hoods raised. These in the brown habits were the catechumens, ready for the waters of baptism, readied by baptism to participate in Christ's death and resurrection.

Huddled against the night air near the walls of the stone church, Monsignor Easton intoned a prayer: "O God, who through your Son bestowed upon the faithful the fire of your glory, sanctify this new fire, we pray."

A metal basin of dry kindling erupted in flame, casting the dark away as Christ did when he rose, trampling down death by death. The Christ candle, a massive pillar of beeswax, was lit from the new fire and borne away from our circle toward a gothic door. The candle was meant to remind us of the pillar of fire that led the children of Israel in their ancient wilderness pilgrimage.

Our journey back to the sanctuary went through a hundred-foot-long chapel, illumined only by the Christ candle and ambient light. I could not make out any of the faces. Where now were the friends I came with?

The procession stopped midway and the monsignor chanted, "May the light of Christ, rising in glory, dispel the darkness of our hearts and minds."

Slowly—very slowly—the pillar of fire led to the sanctuary's entrance, where hundreds not in our procession awaited its arrival.

There were now about a hundred of us in procession, filling the narrow chapel. A baptistry was at the chapel's darkened center, a gap in the press of people where no one stood. Light flickered on the surface of the pool for moments and then was gone.

I could just make out the Christ candle and the clergy, paused ahead before the opening to the sanctuary. There were more prayers and chants that I could hear, though the words were muddled by the distance.

I began to wonder how long I would remain there in shadow when suddenly the pillar of flame began migrating backward, leaping from person to person, as the light from the Christ candle was shared from pilgrim to pilgrim.

The chapel gradually filled with light, making its way back toward those of us who remained in shadow. The growing light illumined gold-limned icons on the chapel walls, and we were made aware that angels and saints surrounded us.

The Light of the World was rekindled, never to go out again. "He who gives his light to all creation is risen." Face after face began to shine, as from one person to the next we were delivered from indistinct silhouette to bright, living color.

The joy of resurrection spread through the room, and then I remembered, once again, as if for the first time as the joy reached me: This fire can never be quenched, this victory can never be undone, this light shines forever. Christ is risen!

ASCENSION

Imagine a human life born into the world the way we all are born into the world, coated in serum and vernix caseosa, now vulnerable to all the things that can bring humans harm.

Imagine a human life born, like most humans, into a poor family with parents who sweat for their daily bread, a human life threatened from the start by political violence.

Imagine a human life lived as a child in exile, in a land where he is a stranger, where a different language is spoken, where all his dearest connections are distant.

Imagine that when Jesus comes home as a young boy to the village of his parents, people stare at him, whisper "bastard." Schoolboys perhaps taunt Jesus, ask him if Mary knows his real father.

Imagine a human life on whom the Word is so inscribed that the greatest teachers of his day hear in his voice the wisdom that inspires the prophets, that lends its harmony to the Psalter.

Imagine a human life that gradually becomes aware that its life is somehow identical with the Life that makes galaxies and quasars, tulips and sequoias, eagles and panthers, that gives breath to all that flies and swims and crawls, that is one with the architect of atoms and cells, the kindler of stars, the molder of mountains.

The other humans, including his mom and stepdad, are not quite sure what to make of his bewildering humility. He is always putting others first, always waiting on them and everyone in the smallest of ways without caring if anyone notices the kindnesses, or him. At times they feel as though perhaps they ought to bow in reverence because his words and acts are so full of life and hope and healing.

Imagine a human life lived for decades in obscurity, where at the end of most days, muscles tired and achy, Jesus rinses grime from his arms and sets a table for the widowed, vulnerable virgin who brought him into the world, who mentored him in the Scriptures and the Psalter, and now has him alone to protect and provide for her.

Then one day this woman asks him to do for others what he has on occasion done for her—to make wine where there is no wine. And then there is a baptism, and a sojourn in the wilderness, and a transfiguration. The blind see, the lame walk, and the dead live again because his spit and voice and breath are not only human but also divine.

Imagine a human who does not seek equality with God but is among all humans as a servant—more comfortable with being small and out of sight than any one of us. Imagine a human life that refuses the sword and tells us to love our enemies. Imagine a life that does human things divinely and divine things humanly.

Imagine that living this kind of human life leads the church of his time and the politicians of his moment to plot against him and to snuff out his way of becoming human, to shame anyone in the future from even trying to be human as God is human by nailing his way of being human to an instrument of torture and shame.

Imagine a human who forgives our entire species even as we reject and despise and murder our God.

Imagine that when this human dies from our violence he does not stay dead but in death and beyond it he stays human. This human so rearranges the structures of death that they are now instead a portal to the life of God for everyone who dies with him, his death now the way by which we all become human.

Imagine a human who journeys to hell with the dead and preaches to those bound in chains, that as he speaks the fetters that held the dead in death are broken by love.

Imagine that the human life I have just described in all the ways I have described it appears embodied again after death, freed from death, liberated from any threat that can limit his promises to us and to the world.

Imagine that what it means to live this sort of life and to die this sort of death is to ascend—to be in eternity the measure of what it means to be God and what it means to be human.

And despite all appearances to the contrary, his way of being human, his way of humility, is now the way things are with the world, and now death has no power over his ascended life or ours.

His humility causes our humanity to ascend with him so that right now what is truest about you and me is that our lives are hidden with Christ in God, that we are seated in Christ next to the Father, that we are in him there, and that he is in us here, and that with him we are one with the Father by the Spirit.

These are only some facets of the mystery called ascension. It's that complex, neglected, and beautiful reality Christians trust and should celebrate more: that God descends to become human and that God ascends to *remain human*.

It turns out that we *can* imagine all of this, as many down the centuries have, thanks to the Scriptures and the prophetic witness of the church, because the human God shows up among us in precisely these ways, and when at last we see him in his passion, we see the Father.

Jesus appears among his disciples after his passion bearing signs of actual-yet-somehow-transfigured wounds and says, "Why are you frightened, and why do doubts arise in your hearts? Look at my hands and my feet; see that it is I myself. Touch me and see, for a ghost does not have flesh and bones as you see that I have" (Luke 24:38–39).

After forty days and nights in which he opens their minds to read the Scriptures and breaks bread with the women and men who come to trust his way of being human, the scarred-and-sacred body of Jesus Christ, a body that in those forty days feasts on fish and honeycomb, ascends into what it means to be God in eternity, forever taking all the good and hard memories of embodiment.

Jesus remembers the ecstatic gladness of wine and bread with friends, that odd mixture of cold and thirst in the desert night, the taste of water from a deep well, the scent of a crocus, and the haunting sound of mourners.

We worship a God who remembers what it is like to die a human death, and all his life and all his death ascend with our Lord Jesus Christ.

As the human who exists beyond the touch of death, whose nail-marked, resurrected body is our death's antidote, as the everlasting human who remembers all our faces, the ascending Son of God keeps his promise to raise us with him—a promise he makes as the firstborn of a new creation and as the firstborn from the dead.

In a homily for ascension, Rowan Williams says that Jesus speaks to the Father in a human voice, takes human language into heaven so that it is "heard at the very center of the burning heart of reality."[1]

Can Jesus take *all* human conversations into the precincts of heaven? Really? Williams brings Augustine's sermons on the Psalms into the conversation, citing the saint's concern that they "are full of rude, angry, violent, hateful remarks; they contain protests against God, and spectacular ill-wishing against human beings."[2]

Why do we bring all of that into our worship? Augustine wonders. Should we not refrain from anger and doubt when talking to God? Well, Augustine reminds us, Jesus in his life among us prays *these very prayers* to the Father.

Williams's sermon is so laden with the Spirit that it's valuable to read it at length:

> Jesus hears all the words we speak—words of pain and protest and rage and violence. He hears them and he takes them and in the presence of God the Father he says, "This is the humanity I have brought home. It's not a pretty sight; it's not edifying and impressive and heroic, it's just real: real and needy and confused," and here it is (this complicated humanity) brought home to heaven, dropped into the burning heart of God—for healing and for transformation.
>
> Jesus has gone before us into the darkest places of human reality. He has picked up the sounds that he hears. And think of what those sounds are: the quiet cries of the abused child . . . the cry of the hungry and the forgotten. He hears the human beings that nobody else hears. And he calls to us to say, "You listen too." He makes his own the cynical dismissal of faith by the sophisticated, and sees through it to the underlying need. He makes his own the joy and celebration and thanksgiving of human beings going about their routine work and finding their fulfilment in ordinary prosaic, bog-standard love and faithfulness. All of that is taken "to the throne of Godhead, / to the Father's breast." All of that on the throne of eternity in the burning heart of truth and reality.[3]

There are so many things to say about what all of this means for every human, what ascension means for God with us and what ascension means for us with God.

Christ ascends to be present in the world anywhere anyone is hungry or thirsty, everywhere anyone is sick or in prison (behind real walls or imagined ones), everywhere anyone is naked of all help and comfort and confidence, as we all are now or anyway will be in the end.

It is also Christ who acts and speaks when humans proclaim the gospel, heal the sick, visit prisoners, care for the poor, release captives, forgive enemies, gather to celebrate the Eucharist, and so on. Jesus in glory is the head of his body, and we his crucified body are the fullness of Christ on the earth.

Ascension means that the sort of power our crucified Lord reveals in the moment of his greatest humiliation is the foundation of every genuine strength. All other ways and means and ends of power are weighed in the balance and found wanting by the weakness of our battered and broken God outside the city walls.

Ascension means that the sort of power our crucified Lord reveals in the moment of his greatest humiliation is the foundation of every genuine strength.

Ascension means this same Jesus governs the globe, no matter how certain a tyrant or court or junta is in their actions or judgments. All their works are passing away.

Christ crucified is Lord, and all temporal rulers and spiritual powers are judged as inadequate, as potential false gods. There is no Lord on earth but the One who is among us as servant, Jesus Christ. Jesus discloses a God who rules all things by a stunning humility. His power is disclosed in poverty, is revealed in surrender and trust.

Ascension means that Someone who knows what it is like to be limited by time and embodiment and hunger and anxiety and rejection and torture and pain and betrayal and thirst and contingency—who knows being human from the inside out—is present in God when we pray, and this Someone knows our every petition and our every experience as one of us who is with us in everything before we ask.

Ascension means that human nature is seated at God's right hand and no one needs to impatiently grasp for divinity again, as did Adam, for Christ has divinized human nature by his suffering. Creatureliness is godliness in Jesus the Son, and humans by grace participate in that union forged in the fire of the cross.

Athanasius says that death has caused the image of our crucified Lord to fade from the bodies on which it was inscribed, that Christ comes to renew the lines and colors of his image on and in us like a master restorationist (*On the Incarnation* 14). The ascended Jesus is at work on and in you by the Spirit, bringing his vibrant hues and sharp lines back to their original magnificence.

Ascension—that the human Jesus is now seated where God is, also *as* God—means that the One who is present to only one or a few or a multitude at once in the Gospels can now be present to everyone, present everywhere, present to everything all the time by the Spirit.

As the body of Christ enters heaven, his body can now be present in bread and wine on a million tables, be embodied in a tiny group of his followers who gather in secret amid tyranny and violence. Christ's body can show up in the person we encounter on the street asking for our help whose need is actually our help, lie helpless in the person we visit in the hospital whose condition reminds us that we too are sick even when all seems well. Christ can inhabit a convict bound by chains whose penitentiary dispels the illusion that any of us are yet free, or appear in an immigrant with callused hands whose labor puts food in our mouths.

And it is this wounded God with human memories, whose rule of resurrection overcomes death, whose rule of forgiveness overcomes sin, whose rule of welcome overcomes estrangement, who takes us (and all our conversations) up with him into heaven.

By the ascension of Jesus on the throne of the tree of pain and sorrows, by his sacred "I am among you as one who serves" (Luke 22:27), there is Someone in the universe who "fills all in all" (Eph. 1:23).

Where is Jesus now? He is closer to you than you are to yourself and loves you with the same love with which he loves all things, and by his ascension he is in everything, everywhere, all at once.

PENTECOST

The bush on Mount Sinai is saturated with flames—every branch, every stem, every leaf. Yet these flames are unlike any fire seen in creation.

The bush is burning but remains unharmed. The leaves are not turning black, the branches are not withering, not falling to earth or aglow with slow destruction. If anything, the bush is more alive.

The plant is verdant, full of life and moisture; its internal life-giving structures are intact. There is no smoke or smell of burning, but there is somehow an inexplicable, attractive fire. This strange fire that engulfs yet preserves life is what turns the head of Moses and turns our heads.

This fiery sign in the wilderness marks the beginning of Israel's exodus, an event that for the first Christians tells the long story of humanity as a miraculous deliverance from death enacted by the faithfulness of God.

Chaim Potok describes Moses in this decisive moment:

> Years have passed since [his] flight from Egypt. The prince is a Bedouin now, in the dusty desert garb of the Sand-Crossers. The inexhaustible black soil of the rich Nile valley, the vast temples, the many gods, the golden palace of the pharaoh, the opulence of

> his youth—all are a vanished dream in the hot, dry, mountainous wilderness with its violent sunlight and shadows, burning days and chilling nights, and the flock that picks at the low leaves of scrub brush and occasional wild grasses that grow in the reddish earth.[1]

The angel of the Lord calls out to Moses from the midst of the flaming blackberry bush. This is not, like Gabriel, an angelic messenger. As we listen to the words of this "angel," it becomes clear that Someone within God is speaking not just *for God* but *as God.*

Moses is told to take off his sandals because he is standing on holy ground—nothing dead can come between the flesh of Moses and the presence of God.

A voice from the bramble declares, "I am the God of your father, the God of Abraham, the God of Isaac, and the God of Jacob" (Exod. 3:6). Moses, we are told, "hid his face, for he was afraid to look *at God*" (3:7, emphasis added). The narrator and Moses agree: This is no less than God speaking, and this God has a face.

God tells Moses from the flaming bush that he has seen the affliction of his people, that he has heard their cries, that he *knows* their pain. God tells Moses that he is sending him to deliver the Hebrews from death (Egypt): "I have come down to help them, pry them loose from the grip of Egypt, get them out of that country" (Exod. 3:8 Message).

"Why me, Lord?" Moses asks. It's not just Moses's question; it's every human's question.

God is terse with Moses (and with us): "I will be with you" (Exod. 3:12) is God's only reply, echoing in the words of Jesus to his disciples at his ascension, "I am with you always, to the end of the age" (Matt. 28:20).

"I will be with you." Moses is asked to trust this. We are asked to trust this. Moses asks to know the name of the God who sends him. The angel of the Lord tells Moses, "I AM WHO I AM" (Exod. 3:14).

John's Gospel records seven "I am" statements spoken out into the world by Jesus:

> "I am the bread of life." (6:35)
> "I am the light of the world." (8:12)
> "I am the gate." (10:9)
> "I am the good shepherd." (10:11)
> "I am the resurrection and the life." (11:25)
> "I am the way and the truth and the life." (14:6)
> "I am the vine." (15:5)

Christ's seven self-identifications help us read Moses, help us experience the burning bush as transfigured by Christ, by God with a face.

When we pray with the Eastern church this connection to Christ is centered in our hearts: "O Virgin . . . Moses, with prophetic eyes, beheld the mystery that was to take place in you, as he saw the bush that burned, yet was not consumed, for, the fire of divinity did not consume your womb."[2]

Moses's moment at the burning bush and the moment of Gabriel's announcement to the virgin are initiations of Passover, are holy ground, are what rescue us from death, and from where God sits, they are the *same moment.*

This story of the burning bush, of the beginning of Passover, is a gospel story.

The first Christians did not pull this way of reading Exodus out of a hat. Paul taught them to read (and to pray) Exodus in this way: "Remember our history, friends, and be warned. All our ancestors were led by the providential Cloud and taken miraculously through the Sea. They went through the waters, in a baptism like ours, as Moses led them from enslaving death to salvation life. They all ate and drank identical food and drink, meals provided daily by God. They drank from the Rock, God's fountain for them that stayed with them wherever they were. And the Rock was Christ" (1 Cor. 10:1–4 Message).

The story of Israel's Passover, their journey through death to resurrection, is our story.

In the Synoptic Gospels, the Sadducees ask Jesus a complicated question about a woman who marries seven brothers, wanting to know whose wife she will be in the resurrection (that, you will remember, they don't believe in).

We tend to focus on Jesus's answer that there are no marriages in the world that is coming to this world and miss Jesus's strong rebuke of the Sadducees for assuming that the seven brothers and their wife are *dead*.

Jesus says they are in God's sight *very much alive*.

To show this, Jesus takes them to our moment with Moses at the fiery bush: "As for the resurrection of the dead, have you not read what was said to you by God, 'I am the God of Abraham, the God of Isaac, and the God of Jacob'?" Then Jesus adds, "He is God not of the dead but of the living" (Matt. 22:31–32). Where God is these long-dead ancestors are among the living who are somehow more alive than we are, not less.

Notice, God takes for granted that what was said to Moses at the burning bush was said somehow also to the Sadducees and—dare we ignore this?—to us, as if we are all there in the deep wilderness with our sandals off.

We *are* in the same story, all of us. And we will all in the end be among the forever alive.

What is the nature of a fire that does not consume what it burns, a fire that is somehow both like and unlike what we know as fire?

God is love and *love is a fire*, a light and heat that consume sin and death without consuming creation or creatures.

The first Christians see and hear the Son of God in the burning bush, in the "angel" that speaks from its center, in the Lord whose face is somehow made visible to Moses in the flames. This humble bramble, low to the ground and of no reputation, reveals the body of God in the lowly humanity of Jesus Christ, and the sacred flame reveals the divine life that suffuses the only begotten's ordinary, frail human dust. Once again, the iron of Christ's flesh becomes known by the properties of fire.

The God of this burning bramble knows the pain of Israel and our pain—*from the inside*, in the flesh of Jesus hanging from a tree. The mystery of Jesus Christ is great: The human things he does reveal his humble divinity, and the divine things he does reveal his vulnerable humanity.

When Jesus speaks with Moses from the midst of the burning bush in the obscurity of the deep wilderness, it is the crucified Lord who speaks.

The deliverance that God accomplishes in the flesh of Jesus, by the Passover he endures on the cross—prefigured in the thorns of the engulfed-but-not-consumed bush—is the defeat of death.

The children of our parish inspire me, bowing as the cross passes them in our gospel procession. They reverence not an instrument of torture but their God. They bow as Moses did before the burning bush, knowing in their bones, as perhaps only children can, that they are somehow on holy ground.

I watch as they make the sign of the cross over themselves, remembering that as we embrace this practice—in the assembly and during the week—our lives are interpreted by the death of God for the life of the world, interpreted by the burning bush.

It's these little ones I have in mind and heart as we remember the words of Jesus: "I have come to cast fire upon the earth, and how I wish it were already ablaze!" (Luke 12:49). In the churches in which many of us were raised, we were taught—explicitly or implicitly—to live in fear of the fire of God. We are not making that mistake as we disciple our children. The first Christians show us a better way of perceiving this divine fire we encounter in the Scriptures and in our lived experiences.

I want our children to trust that they can welcome and embrace the fire of God—to learn that there is no reason to live in terror of the fire that has come from God, that is coming from God right now as we stand on holy ground, and that will come from God in the end.

We welcome the fire of God because we know the character of the God who meets us in the flesh of Jesus Christ. This God comes among us not to destroy humanity but to burn everything out of us that is not of love, that does not have its origin in the divine life. He means to drive out evil. He means to melt the dross.

We welcome the fire of God because we know the character of the God who meets us in the flesh of Jesus Christ.

Like with all healing, deliverance, and reconciliation, there is pain involved in being set free and made well. It is not easy. It is not a cake walk. But it is pure gift.

Humanity became cold when we turned away from Love, and like any object, the further it travels away from the fiery source of its life, the colder it becomes.

Yet there is good news: We are freed from anxiety and fear as we *embrace* the cleansing fire of God. "With its fire, love makes better whatever it has touched," Ambrose of Milan reminds us.[3]

Remember: The burning bush is aflame and entirely engulfed but never consumed by the fire.

Remember: The flames of the fiery furnace do not consume the Hebrew children. The angel—Christ himself—stands with them in the scorching flames, and they emerge from the fire unharmed.

Remember: God makes his ministers flames of fire, and in the end we shine like the sun in the kingdom of heaven.

And so the fire is with us now: The fire that is the Spirit of God—Ambrose describes the fire of Love as having wings—flies through us, consuming whatever is not of Love and trying whatever is good in us in order to purify the good and make it ready for the kingdom.[4]

And we can trust this fire because the fire is the Spirit of the human who is God, who has journeyed through death and hell to bring us back alive with him.

The way you come to have Isaiah's visions of this world recreated—every farm and street and dwelling engulfed by the fire of divine and permanent flourishing, a world where children don't die, where no one must cry for help and no blood is shed, where everyone lives to see and enjoy the good fruit of their labor and nothing is wasted—is first to see in flesh the God who makes this sort of transfiguration credible (Isa. 6; 9; 11; 25; 65).

And here we return to the great beauty and great mystery of the burning bush: God tells Moses that he has always been and always will be known as the God of Abraham, Isaac, and Jacob. God decides to identify himself with the human story, with our story—with the stories of Abraham and Sarah, Isaac and Rebecca, Jacob and Rachel, Moses and Isaiah—and to name himself using *our names.*

This story of a bush and God and Moses is by the Spirit *our story*, is the story of the church as nothing less than the whole human family, is *every human's story.*

By grace, every human can become as this bush: engulfed by the fiery presence of God but unharmed, fully involved by flames that sanctify them, body and soul, burning away everything in them that is not of Love.

The first Christians, some of whom, like Moses, dwelt in the desert, tell this story: "Abba Lot went to see Abba Joseph and said to him, 'Abba as far as I can I say my little office, I fast a little, I pray and meditate, I live in peace and as far as I can, I purify my thoughts. What else can I do?' then the old man stood up and stretched his hands towards heaven. His fingers became like ten lamps of fire and he said to him, 'If you will, you can become all flame.'"[5]

This gift of grace begins for all humans with the sending of the Spirit at Pentecost, as A. W. Tozer describes:

> "And there appeared unto them cloven tongues like as of fire, and it sat upon each of them" (Acts 2:3). That which came upon the disciples in that upper room was nothing less than God himself. . . . The God who had appeared to them as fire throughout all their long history was now dwelling in them as fire. He had moved from without to the interior of their lives. The Shekinah that had once blazed over the mercy seat now blazed on their foreheads as an external emblem of the fire that had invaded their natures. This was Deity giving himself to ransomed humanity. The flame was the seal of a new union. They were now men and women of the Fire.[6]

When Peter preaches on the day of Pentecost, a text from Joel is the prophetic well he draws from to begin to preach the cross: "I will pour out my Spirit on all flesh" (Joel 2:28). The Spirit of Christ is poured out on everyone from the cross (John 19:30), and fifty days later, as Cyril of Jerusalem teaches, Jesus's words about "casting fire upon the earth" find their fulfillment in these men and women (*Catechetical Lectures* 17.8). Christ baptizes them all with fire and the Spirit.

So why doesn't it look like everyone is touched by the cross? Why isn't every human life a witness to the humilities of cruciform love . . . especially, so often, the followers of Jesus? Why do so few seem willing to receive the Spirit of the crucified One? Why is every bush not burning? Why is every meal not a Eucharist?

Remember: Pentecost is not something we humans do; it is something God does. With God all things are possible, and this is the God of all flesh (Jer. 32:27). And all flesh means *all flesh* (*kol balsar*). And so we trust and pray.

We trust there is a human who lives to see this divine fire of Love fall on everyone and everything in every moment of time from the future God promises, our Lord Jesus Christ, who alone can without harm remove the tares from our virtues and harvest the wheat from our vices, who will with sanctifying fire make us the humans he intends us to be.

We wait with anticipation and hope amid the trauma of existence for the healing judgments of God because our encounters with Jesus teach us to trust the fire that is his love.

Pentecost teaches that the presence of the Spirit—and the renewal of humanity that Wisdom brings with her, the revival we need but too rarely desire—is first the gift to understand the story of the world as the story of the cross (Acts 2:22–26), and by the forgiving the cross makes possible to at last *hear* each other.

Babel's imposed diversity of language was a gift that limited for millennia the damage of fallen humanity's collective narcissism and our self-destructive tendencies. Babel's gift of language diversity was also an *expansion* of humanity's cultural possibilities. All the difference in dance and dress and food and color and architecture and sport and art and so on—the beautiful variety of humanity we enjoy—flows from an ancient, gracious dispersal of humanity at Babel.

We are the ones who brought tribal jealousy, prejudice, war, and a grave hardness of heart. We bought the horrific lie of ethnic "superiority" that mars the better intention of God in confusing our speech.

Pentecost is a reversal of Babel where the gospel breaks out of cultural and linguistic boundaries and is heard by all the nations, but it is also a ratification of Babel's blessed diversity. The Spirit that is poured out on all flesh, the Spirit that makes us one in Jesus Christ, opens the ears of collective humanity to understand the message of the cross precisely *within* every distinct and celebrated human language and culture.

The tongues of fire that descend at Pentecost lead to one spiritual language of prayer that is heard by everyone as if it were their mother tongue. The diversity is blessed and the unity is blessed as the healing breath of Jesus spills out on all flesh from his cross. The cross translates our confusion and our animosities into understanding and charity. Pentecost makes the whole world the church.

Whenever we hear what someone is actually saying, when we hear it with our heart, we are experiencing Pentecost.

The Spirit makes possible good hearing—the ability to capture not just the sounds of words but what they mean, especially what they mean for the person who is speaking them.

Eloquence is nothing without comprehension. We can say something as well as we might, but when the Spirit blows on our speech, the miracle of understanding takes place in the persons we are addressing.

God loves the nations. God loves the world. God loves what God makes. But he does not love everything that humans make. Love is not the aim of everything that humans construct, for we yet remain in bondage to the powers of sin and death.

At Pentecost, the Spirit makes us a peculiar people who reflect the Prince of Peace, gives us the mind of Christ, and initiates the everlasting kingdom the Son of God brings, where swords and spears, drones and cruise missiles are beaten into gardening tools.

When by the Spirit we ignore satanic voices that hinder us from taking up our cross, we with Christ become walking, talking trees of life, aflame with the fire of God but not destroyed, made ready to participate in his deliverance of those who all their lifetimes are enslaved by the fear of death, made ready to love our enemies, made ready to preserve the creation God loves.

There are burning bushes all around us if we have eyes to see. May we take off our sandals, enter the silence of the deep wilderness, and hear what God has to say to us about the end of death.

VULNERABLE

At the end of all things, Jesus comes back as the same person we meet in the Gospels—the same human who healed the children of soldiers and whispered storms into silence, the same God who ate with sex workers and died with thieves, the dying slave who pardons his killers and pours out his Spirit on all flesh, the same person who is a threat not to any person or the creation but only to the evil in us and in the world.

When at last we are blessed to see God, it would seem wise to prepare ourselves to see Someone who appears as the child or as the crucified, for there is no other God besides the tiny infant in Bethlehem, besides the dead convict hanging outside the walls of Jerusalem.

The appearance of God in the end, the appearance that brings all humans to their knees and causes the trees to shout for joy, is the unveiling of a mystery: a humility we do not know, a mercy we have not seen, a love we have not anticipated.

The church's gradual and at times nearly complete break with the pattern of her Lord and with the first Christians on the question of war is a scandal. From the Crusades onward (including our own moment), Christians brook no competition in shedding the blood of their enemies and shedding each other's blood.

Jacques Ellul says that "when satan offers to him all the kingdoms of the earth, Jesus refuses, but the church accepts."[1]

Dorothy Day, a contemporary practitioner of deep Christianity, uses the words of Jesus about mercy to help us: "You just need to look at what the gospel asks and what war does. The Gospel asks that we feed the hungry, give drink to the thirsty, clothe the naked, welcome the homeless, visit the prisoner, and perform acts of mercy. War does all the opposite. It makes my neighbor hungry, thirsty, homeless, a prisoner and sick. The Gospel asks us to take up our cross. War asks us to lay the cross on others."[2]

And so it comes to this: Either we believe finally that love is stronger than death, and the way of the cross stronger than the way of the sword, or we do not. Do we trust the cross or violence?

Our Lord trusted the way of the cross.

At some point before the end of history, will the church return to Jesus and the first Christians and put her money where her creed is?

Either we trust that the cross and resurrection reveal the way to become human as God is human in the flesh of Jesus Christ, or we believe in the will to power, in horses and chariots, like most peoples in history.

Christ followers of the first couple centuries sought the kingdom of heaven. They did not seek rescue in the state or in the cult of empire.

Christian ambition for the fallen order of things—for the Ring of Power, as J. R. R. Tolkien aptly names the lust for control in *The Lord of the Rings*—is healed by a vision of Jesus Christ, who says, "Come to me, all you who are weary and are carrying heavy burdens, and I will give you rest. . . . For I am gentle and humble in heart" (Matt. 11:28–29).

The first Christians represent a turn in human existence when for more than three hundred years these women and men joined

Jesus on the way of the cross—without insurgencies, without rebellions, without riots, without wars. Their teacher Tertullian taught them that "Christ, in disarming Peter, [disarmed] every soldier."[3] They were fully immersed in our Lord's way of dying to become human. They chose the way of the cross. Athanasius, in describing the courage of the martyrs in Rome's arenas, reports that for them "no longer is death fearsome but all believers in Christ tread on it as nothing, and would rather choose to die than deny their faith in Christ."[4]

They are the first sustained movement of nonviolence in history, and their imitation of Jesus still stands as a great witness to the authenticity of the gospel.

Since Stephen, seventy million have perished—more than half of whom died in the twentieth century, two million of whom perished since 2001—while trusting in the crucified God.[5] Should this remnant have taken a more realistic or utilitarian path; should they have taken up arms to make the world Christian by force? To ask seems a blasphemy of the Holy Spirit. These followers of Jesus who were looking for a transfigured world had a different country in their hearts. They trusted that God is on the side of humanity, on the side of his creation, that God is for all continents and peoples and cultures, that God is with and for everyone, everywhere.

These followers of Jesus who were looking for a transfigured world had a different country in their hearts.

We can keep defending ourselves and protecting our lives and fighting by worldly means, and perhaps God will allow us to do so for a very long time, for something close to the "world without end" we invoke in the liturgy. But what if to reach perfection, to reach "the measure of the full stature of Christ" (Eph. 4:13), the Spirit invites us to lay down our collective life for the life of the world according to the pattern of Jesus, as the first Christians did, and see God raise us together with the glorious, never-ending temple of the Son on the third day?

Is there a final moment in history when, instead of fighting, instead of taking up arms against the penultimate Hitler or the final ISIS or whatever form death's last great tyranny takes, the church visibly rejects the means and powers of this world, this privilege of self-defense, our idolatry of weapons, and wills instead to beat our swords and spears into farming tools, chooses to trust not our armaments, our anger, or our right to stand up for ourselves but the humility and weakness of God in Jesus Christ to vindicate us in order to globally manifest an already-accomplished defeat of evil on Golgotha?

What if the end comes only after a worldwide crucifixion of the body of Christ, in which after great sacrifice in imitation of her Lord she dies and rises from the ashes of her demise by the Spirit, and God is finally all in all because the cruciform pattern of love that governs the universe and holds all things together and gives all living things breath has been confirmed in a peculiar crucified and resurrected people with Christ as her head?

The life of the unborn, the prisoner, the refugee, the "useless"—the poorest among us—cannot be secured in any ultimate sense by the power of pen or sword, much less by activism, but only by the foolishness of the cross, only by a world-converting love that is willing to die that everyone might live.

Jesus says our lives and the life of the world will be made secure not by defending our lives or trying to hold on to our privilege but by giving up our lives so that the world might live. For most of us, most of the time, that means not persecution or death but the preferring of others; noticing and responding to our neighbor who is in need; doing what we can to bear their burden while we are carrying our own load; allowing ourselves to be interrupted, inconvenienced; living simply, quietly, patiently, sacrificially; not insisting on our own way. We pine for resurrection, we run rehearsals for the opening of all tombs, we trust that love is stronger than death, we glimpse Easter in the ashes of this Holy Saturday world.

In the moment of Christ's death, it is *deep humility* that splits the rocks and opens the earth; that rends the vast curtain of the Temple from top to bottom; that raises long-dead persons from their tombs.

It is *deep humility* that the centurion and his party of soldiers witness in the dead body of Jesus on the tree; that helps them see for the first time that the way to be human and the way to be God is to die in this way so that the world might live; that bids them to exclaim, "Truly this man was God's Son"; that invites them to cross-bearing love in a world that crucifies.

Sometimes our witness to Christ becomes a martyrdom. When a Christian or group of Christians dies because they trust that Christ is the revelation of what it means to be God and what it means to be human, their deaths are a sign in a dying world that love is stronger than death.

Resurrection is what follows, but resurrection is not about returning to fight worldly means of power with the powers known to this world. For Jesus (and for us), to live again beyond death is to be the peace and forgiveness that mend the world.

We will all die in the end, and we will die (in various ways) while we live. The promise of the gospel is that when we die we won't stay dead, that now because of what happened to death in the death of our brother, Jesus Christ, to die—daily and at the end of our lives—is to begin actually and finally to live.

Because we are the body of Christ, our deaths are like the death of Jesus, a great humility accepted voluntarily for the life of the world: "There is no greater love than to lay down one's life for one's friends" (John 15:13 NLT), even friends that in the moment of our deaths look a lot like enemies.

And if you strike us down, what we become by grace are partakers of the essential essence of God: everlasting loving-kindness.

What we become is indestructible love.

ONE

Paul is under house arrest in Rome for "speak[ing] the mystery of Christ" (Col. 4:3), but his vision of Christ is so magnificent that it causes him to experience his hardships differently.

What Paul sees and hears of Jesus gives him a sure and certain hope that his sufferings are not the last thing but the next-to-last thing. Paul is confident even in his pain that a world is coming that transfigures and heals all suffering.

At the beginning of his letter to the Colossians, Paul reaches for a hymn of the first Christians (Col. 1:15–20), a song they sang in their gatherings. The hymn says that Christ, the visibility of the invisible God, not only creates *everything* that exists, but holds everything that exists together—from the invisible particles that make up every visible thing to the largest stars in the farthest regions of the cosmos.

The hymn says that everything of God was present in Christ, who we've learned is human without losing anything divine and divine without losing anything human. The song says that Christ, as the creator and sustainer of all things, is the first in creation to live beyond death so that he can bring everything in creation—all things!—back into union with God.

The hymn says that *everything* in heaven and on earth is *now* reconciled in Jesus Christ by the "blood of his cross" (Col. 1:20).

Paul found that pondering Jesus Christ in all things gave him space and time to be human as God is human. Paul found that speaking the mystery made living as the human God lives thinkable and doable. When we trust that Jesus Christ is making all things well, we can endure and we can hope and we can love in the middle of the hardest things at the hardest times.

Every attempt to speak or write the mystery of Jesus Christ falls short, as George MacDonald confesses: "To know Christ is an infinitely higher thing than to know all theology, all that is said about his person, or babbled about his work."[1]

The Christ Hymn of the first Christians says all that I have tried but failed to say in this book, and I thank God for that failure. Even so, I will try one last time to say what can never be said adequately about the One who encounters us in Jesus Christ:

> *The One who is timeless and changeless and all-powerful makes himself vulnerable and contingent to all the natural forces he breathed into existence, and in time and space—his creatures—he lies helpless in a feed box, dependent on Mary and Joseph for nourishment and shelter. Needlessly, he makes himself needy. He suffers without suffering the fact that he suffers.*
>
> *The One who is the origin of all things and who holds all things in existence—galactic to microscopic—is the carpenter from Nazareth. The One who made the Pleiades and Orion now sets beams and crafts doors with Joseph. The splinters in his little hands foreshadow deeper wounds.*
>
> *The One who baptizes with the Holy Spirit and fire is bathed by his mother and later baptized with water to draw*

close to every imperfect human brother and sister, to identify with our brokenness so humanity can be united to our baptized and baptizing God.

The One who does not eat the flesh of bulls or drink the blood of goats is now in Jesus a hungering, thirsting creature, set to fast in the Judaean desert, to feast at table with strangers and friends.

The One who owns the cattle on a thousand hills and is the Lord of angels is now homeless and a sojourner, cloaked against the cold night and alone, tempted by satan, all without in any way losing touch with or care for each and every last thing he has made in all the epochs of time and all the ages of eternity.

The One who embodies the law dines with tax collectors, prostitutes, and winos; he is at home with them, not setting them at ease with anything that binds them but loving them toward freedom.

The One who is a consuming fire of holy otherness beyond all comprehension, who dwells in light inaccessible from before time and forever, embraces and kisses lepers, the blind, and all who are ritually unclean. Jesus, wrapped in the luminous dark of the Spirit, shines on all who sit in darkness and the shadow of death.

The only One who is without sin forgives as he draws in the sand, throws no stones, and condemns no one. This crucified God does not crucify.

The eternal One hangs on a tree as the sands of his mortal life seep from the hourglass until "it is finished."

The One who knows no sin becomes sin, bearing the sins of the whole world, bearing them away. White-collar sins. Red-light-district sins. Stained-glass sins. The desperate sins of the hopeless. Secret sins. Brazen sins. Christian sins. My sins. And he does not merely forgive. Jesus heals all wounds.

Undoes all damage. Rights all wrongs. Dethrones the powers. Binds the devil. Obliterates the almost endless banality and cruelty of evil, bringing it at long last to a fitting end.

The One who holds everything in movement and life is an indestructible Love in human flesh that has no beginning and no end precisely because our human God has been crucified. And this is how in the face of all our crucifixions he has the authority in the face of death—his enemy and ours—to give us this invitation: Do not be afraid!

These and other sentences like them are what we mean when we confess that the Word became flesh and dwelt among us.

Humanity may have misplaced her brightest lantern, may have forgotten about its Bridegroom altogether, but the uncreated light of the crucified One shines on in the darkness and the darkness cannot overcome it.

ACKNOWLEDGMENTS

This book is dedicated to my paternal grandmother, Lela Stepp Tanner, whose devotion to Jesus illumined my young life. On the many weekends I stayed with her and my grandfather Lawrence, she read the Scriptures and devotional books to me in the evening, and we prayed. She could do anything, and her heart in all the things she did was serving others. Somewhere in the communion of saints, she is glad this book exists.

This book could also be dedicated to the four black women who were my primary school teachers and who above anyone else blessed me with a love for words and for reading, and to teachers and friends who most help me read the Scriptures in the way that I do: Neil Brant, Jeff Zippi, Dennis McNutt, Hugh Morken, Joel Budd, Bill Epperson, Thomas Oden, Patrick Henry Reardon, S. M. Hutchens, Robert Jenson, and Fleming Rutledge.

The title of this work was first suggested by the late, wonderful Jack Heaslip in a letter describing what our conversations meant to him, how they kept "the vulnerable God" in the forefront of his imagination. I am grateful for Jack, who showed a lot of us what church looks like outside the walls of a church.

I wish to thank friends who read all or parts of this book and offered advice and encouragement: Winn Collier, Cherith Fee Nordling, Brad Jersak, Julie Canlis, Ben Myers, and John Behr, especially Andrew Arndt and Daniel Taylor, who commented on most or all the draft chapters. More than anyone in this respect, I wish to thank Chris Green, who gave the entire book a close reading and whose insights and suggestions are essential throughout.

I am grateful for audiences who have listened to our concerns about the gospel and responded: the Multiply student group at Hart Middle School; divinity students at Western Theological Seminary and participants in the annual Doxology conference at its Eugene Peterson Center; participants in the summer program at the Calvin Center for Christian Worship; clergy and laity of the Charismatic Episcopal Church meeting in convocation; and above all the community that attend in-person and online events of the Open Table Conference, led by its tireless founder, John MacMurray.

A special thanks to my writing friends in the Kindred Collective and the Squad. You are a constant grace to me.

Blessings on Katelyn Beaty and Mick Silva for encouraging me through a long illness that fell in the late stages of refining this book. A good editor is hard to find, and Katelyn and Mick are as good as it possibly gets. Melinda Timmer, Celina Sourbeer, and Julie Zahm clarified and cleaned up my mess. This book is the result of the gifts and care of the Brazos team.

Stephanie Smith has my gratitude for seeing the heart of this book and for championing it. A profound thanks to Estee Zandee for believing and converting the right people, and to Andrea Heineke for having my back in the literary world. Cathleen Falsani knew this book was in me and helped coax these contemplations into reality. Brian Zahnd wrote the illuminating foreword and is among those friends whose encouragements most inspired these pages.

The people of Holy Redeemer are most responsible for these words, because my love for them and for Jesus has led to these pages existing at all.

My deepest affection to my wife, Debbie, and our seven children and four grandchildren. They are always with me even when the work has not gone well. We thank God for that failure.

All praise to the Living Word.

NOTES

FOREWORD

1. The full text of the Nicene Creed is available at https://www.anglicancommunion.org/media/109020/Nicene-Creed.pdf.

MYSTERY

1. Sacred Arts@SVOTS, "Arvo Pärt at St. Vladimir's Seminary—From My Musical Diaries," commencement speech given at St. Vladimir's Seminary, May 31, 2014, Vimeo, posted June 9, 2017, 6 min., 48 sec., https://vimeo.com/221011528.

BASIN

1. Origen, *Against Celsus* 6.75, in *The Ante-Nicene Fathers*, vol. 4, trans. Frederick Crombie (Christian Literature, 1885), 608.

2. Sergius Bulgakov, *The Sophiology of Death. Essays on Eschatology: Personal, Political, and Universal*, trans. Roberto J. De La Noval (Cascade Books, 2021), 132.

FLESH

1. Lucy Peppiatt, *Rediscovering Scripture's Vision for Women: Fresh Perspectives on Disputed Texts* (IVP Academic, 2019), 30.

2. Irenaeus, *Against Heresies* 3.22.4, in *The Ante-Nicene Fathers*, vol. 1, *The Apostolic Fathers*, ed. Alexander Roberts and James Donaldson (Christian Literature, 1885), 455.

DRAGON

1. Jason Micheli (@JASONMICHELI), "Veiled in Bread, the Godhead See," Substack, December 24, 2022, https://jasonmicheli.substack.com/p/veiled-in-bread-the-godhead-see.

2. Pope Francis, *Christmas at the Nativity* (New City, 2023), 19–20.

HIDDEN

1. Dietrich Bonhoeffer, *Ethics*, trans. Reinhard Krauss, Charles C. West, and Douglas W. Scott (Fortress, 2005), 235–36.

2. Dietrich Bonhoeffer, *The Cost of Discipleship*, trans. R. H. Fuller and Irmgard Booth (Simon & Schuster, 1959), 177–78.

BAPTISM

1. Dietrich Bonhoeffer, *Ethics*, trans. Reinhard Krauss, Charles C. West, and Douglas W. Scott (Fortress, 2005), 275.

2. This observation is from Judith Couchman, *The Mystery of the Cross: Bringing Ancient Images to Life* (InterVarsity, 2009), 88.

TEMPTATION

1. Chromatius, *Tractate on Matthew* 14.2, in *Ancient Christian Commentary on Scripture, New Testament, Matthew 1–13*, vol. 1A, trans. Manlio Simonetti (InterVarsity, 2001), 58.

2. John Behr's translation of *On the Incarnation* 54 from an online exchange with John Behr, the author, and some colleagues hosted by the Open Table Conference, March 4, 2026.

3. George MacDonald, *George MacDonald: An Anthology*, ed. C. S. Lewis (HarperCollins, 2001), 14–15.

4. Malcolm Guite, *The Word in the Wilderness: A Poem a Day for Lent and Easter* (Canterbury Press, 2014), 18.

SYNAGOGUE

1. Robert Jenson, "Scripture's Authority in the Church," in *The Triune Story: Collected Essays on Scripture*, ed. Brad East (Oxford University Press, 2019), 118.

2. Brian Zahnd, *Sinners in the Hands of a Loving God: The Scandalous Truth of the Very Good News* (WaterBrook, 2017), 50.

3. Augustine, *On Christian Doctrine* 3.15, in *Nicene and Post-Nicene Fathers*, ser. 1, vol. 2., trans. J. F. Shaw (Christian Literature, 1887), 563.

PHOTINI

1. John Behr, *John the Theologian and His Paschal Gospel: A Prologue to Theology* (Oxford University Press, 2019), 146.

2. Young Oceans, "*Vidi Aquam*," YouTube, June 23, 2015, http://www.youtube.com/watch?v=srhpNd8nh8A.

EVERYONE

1. Gregory of Nyssa, *Second Homily on the Song of Songs*, *Patrologia Graeca*, vol. 44 (Migne, 1858), 765.

2. Herbert McCabe, *Law, Love, and Language* (Sheed and Ward, 1968), 119.

3. Dietrich Bonhoeffer, *God Is in the Manger: Reflections on Advent and Christmas*, ed. Jana Riess, trans. O. C. Dean Jr. (Westminster John Knox, 2010), 2.

4. John Behr, *Becoming Human: Meditations on Christian Anthropology in Word and Image* (St. Vladimir's Seminary Press, 2013), 1.

5. John Behr, "Irenaeus' Gratitude and Derrida's Gift: Time, Death, Life," *Philosophy, Theology, and the Sciences* 9, no. 1 (2022): 5–21.

SHEPHERD

1. A traditional prayer attributed to John of Damascus.

2. Michael Ramsey, *God, Christ, and the World: A Study in Contemporary Theology* (Morehouse-Barlow, 1969), 41.

3. David Bentley Hart, *The Doors of the Sea: Where Was God in the Tsunami?* (Eerdmans, 2005), 86–87.

4. *Shemot Rabbah* 2:2, in *Midrash Rabbah*, trans. H. Freedman and Maurice Simon (Soncino, 1939), 49.

5. Rabbi Schneerson's words are as quoted in William Lobdell, "Judaism's Thriving Concern," *Los Angeles Times*, June 22, 2004, https://www.latimes.com/archives/la-xpm-2004-jun-22-me-chabad22-story.html.

HEALER

1. Ben Myers, "Atonement: The Birth Narratives & Incarnation," YouTube, October 21, 2025, 5 min., 8 sec., https://youtu.be/PRZduFnaEow?si=B2_cekD3xBm63k1q.

2. Dorothy L. Sayers, "The Greatest Drama Ever Staged," Plough, April 10, 2020, https://www.plough.com/en/topics/culture/holidays/easter-readings/the-greatest-drama-ever-staged.

3. Karl Rahner, *The Great Church Year* (Crossroad, 2001), 62.

4. Gregory Nazianzen, Letter to Cledonius 101, in *Nicene and Post-Nicene Fathers*, ser. 2, vol. 7., trans. C. G. Browne and J. E. Swallow (Christian Literature, 1894), 440, (emphasis added, translation modified by Marcelo P. Souza).

5. Jürgen Moltmann, *The Way of Jesus Christ*, trans. Margaret Kohl (Fortress, 1995), 98–99.

6. Athanasius, *On the Incarnation*, trans. John Behr (St. Vladimir's Seminary Press, 2011), 95.

7. *A Brief History of Time*, directed by Errol Morris (Janus Films, 1991).

8. Ambrose of Milan, *On Isaac and the Soul* 8.77, in *The Fathers of the Church*, vol. 65, trans. Michael P. McHugh (Catholic University of America Press, 1972), 60–61.

MOUNTAIN

1. J. R. R. Tolkien, *The Lord of the Rings*, vol. 1, *The Fellowship of the Ring* (Houghton Mifflin, 1982), 393.

2. Oliver Sacks, *Hallucinations* (Alfred A. Knopf, 2012), 109–10.

3. G. K. Chesterton, *The Man Who Was Thursday: A Nightmare* (Penguin Classics, 2011), 145.

CLOUD

1. Origen, *A Commentary of Origen on the Gospel of Matthew*, vol. 1, trans. Roland E. Heine (Oxford University Press, 2018), 125.

2. Karl Barth, *Church Dogmatics* IV/4, trans. Geoffrey W. Bromiley, ed. Geoffrey W. Bromiley and T. F. Torrance (T&T Clark, 1969), 13–14.

JERUSALEM

1. John Behr, *Becoming Human: Meditations on Christian Anthropology in Word and Image* (St. Vladimir's Seminary Press, 2013), i.

2. Behr, *Becoming Human*, 1.

3. Bede the Venerable, *Homilies on the Gospels*, 2 vols., trans. L. T. Martin and D. Hurst (Cistercian Publications, 1990), 2:26–27.

4. Azriel David Fastag, "Ani Ma'amin," arr. Paul Caldwell and Sean Ivory, trans. Joshua Jacobson (Earthsongs, 2005).

SUPPER

1. Nicholas Cabasilas, *The Life in Christ*, trans. Carmino J. De Catanzaro (St. Vladimir's Seminary Press, 1974), 122.

2. Ignatius of Antioch, "Letter to the Romans," in *The Letters*, trans. Alistair Stewart (St. Vladimir's Seminary Press, 2013), 67–71, translation of third phrase modified by John Behr.

3. Theophilus of Alexandria, *Message of the Fathers of the Church*, vol. 7, *The Eucharist*, trans. Daniel J. Sheerin (Michael Glazier, 1986), 154.

4. Chris Green and Kenneth Tanner, hosts, *Crackers & Grape Juice*, podcast, episode 93, "Robert Jenson: Don't Thank Me, Thank the Holy Spirit," March 14, 2017, https://crackersnjuice.substack.com/p/episode-92-robert-jenson-dont-thank-45e.

5. Cyril of Alexandria, *Commentary on John*, vol. 2, *Ancient Christian Texts*, trans. David R. Maxwell (InterVarsity, 2015), 107.

6. Hippolytus, *Against Noetus* 8, in *Ante-Nicene Fathers*, vol. 5, ed. Alexander Roberts and James Donaldson (Christian Literature, 1886), 230.

7. *The Passion of the Christ*, directed by Mel Gibson (Icon Productions, 2004).

8. Chris Green, *The Wound of Unknowing: A Dogmatic Christology* (Baylor University Press, forthcoming).

CROSS

1. John Behr, *The Mystery of Christ: Life in Death* (St. Vladimir's Seminary Press, 2006), 90.

2. Edward Shillito, "Jesus of the Scars," *Plough*, May 26, 2022, https://www.plough.com/en/topics/devotional-reading/jesus-of-the-scars.

3. John Stott, *The Cross of Christ* (InterVarsity, 2006), 326–27. The internal quotation is from P. T. Forsyth, *The Justification of God* (Duckworth, 1916), 32.

4. Dietrich Bonhoeffer, *Ethics*, trans. Reinhard Krauss, Charles C. West, and Douglas W. Scott (Fortress, 2005), 84.

5. Brian Zahnd, *The Unvarnished Jesus: A Lenten Journey* (Spello, 2019), 187.

6. Herbert McCabe, *God Matters* (Continuum, 1987), 93, 97.

7. Chris Green, *All Things Beautiful: An Aesthetic Christology* (Baylor University Press, 2021), 62.

8. Chris Green, "God Is Not a Sacrifice: A Review of Katherine Sonderegger's *Systematic Theology*, Volume 2," *The Other Journal* 33 (Spring 2022): https://theotherjournal.com/2022/02/review-sonderegger-systematic-theology-volume-2.

9. Chris Green, *The Fire and the Cloud: A Biblical Christology* (Baylor University Press, 2024), 44.

10. Stanley Hauerwas, *Fully Alive: The Apocalyptic Humanism of Karl Barth* (University of Virginia Press, 2022), 104.

11. Sharad Yadav, email to author, October 19, 2025.

DEAD

1. David Bentley Hart, *The Doors of the Sea: Where Was God in the Tsunami?* (Eerdmans, 2005), 100–101.

2. Hart, *Doors of the Sea*, 103–4.

3. Selected Liturgical Hymns, "Paschal Troparion," Orthodox Church in America, https://www.oca.org/orthodoxy/prayers/selected-liturgical-hymns.

4. John Behr, "The Christian Art of Dying," *Sobornost* 35, nos. 1–2 (2013): 141 (emphasis original).

BURIED

1. Thomas Lynch, *The Undertaker: Life Studies from the Dismal Trade* (Norton, 1997), 22 (emphasis added).

2. Eric Peterson, phone conversation with author, March 23, 2023.

3. Johannes Baptist Metz, *Poverty of Spirit* (Paulist Press, 1998), 10.

4. Gregory Nazianzen, *Oration* 45.28, in *Festal Orations*, trans. Nonna Verna Harrison (St. Vladimir's Seminary Press, 2008), 189.

5. Robert Farrar Capon, *The Foolishness of Preaching* (Eerdmans, 1997), 107.

6. Elder Sophrony of Essex to Oliviér Clement, in *Taizé: A Meaning to Life* (GIA Publications, 1997), 80.

7. Julian of Norwich, *Showings* (Paulist Press, 1978), 274–75.

MARY

1. C. S. Lewis, *The Lion, the Witch and the Wardrobe* (HarperCollins, 1994), 163.

RESURRECTION

1. Thomas Lynch, *The Undertaker: Life Studies from the Dismal Trade* (Norton, 1997), 21.

2. John Henry Newman, Sermon 21, in *Parochial and Plain Sermons*, vol. 1 (Rivingtons, 1868), 273.

3. Frederick Buechner, *Wishful Thinking: A Theological ABC* (HarperOne, 1973), 51.

4. Serene Jones, "Reverend, You Say the Virgin Birth Is 'a Bizarre Claim'?," interview by Nicholas Kristof, *New York Times*, April 20, 2019, https://www.nytimes.com/2019/04/20/opinion/sunday/christian-easter-serene-jones.html.

5. Chris Green, *All Things Beautiful: An Aesthetic Christology* (Baylor University Press, 2021), 115.

6. Greville MacDonald, *George MacDonald and His Wife* (George Allen & Unwin Ltd., 1924), 173.

ASCENSION

1. Rowan Williams, "A Sermon by the Archbishop of Canterbury at the Ascension Day Sung Eucharist," Dr. Rowan Williams 104th Archbishop of Canterbury, May 21, 2009, https://web.archive.org/web/20240616123324/https://rowanwilliams.archbishopofcanterbury.org/articles.php/883/a-sermon-by-the-archbishop-of-canterbury-at-the-ascension-day-sung-eucharist.html.

2. Williams, "A Sermon by the Archbishop of Canterbury."

3. Williams, "A Sermon by the Archbishop of Canterbury."

PENTECOST

1. Chaim Potok, *Wanderings: Chaim Potok's History of the Jews* (Ballantine, 1983), 123.

2. *Octoechoes; or, The Book of Eight Tones: A Primer Containing the Sunday Service in Eight Tones* (Monastery of the Myrhh-Bearing Women, 2005), 31.

3. Ambrose of Milan, *On Isaac and the Soul* 8.77, in *The Fathers of the Church*, vol. 65, trans. Michael P. McHugh (Catholic University of America Press, 1972), 61.

4. Ambrose of Milan, *On Isaac and the Soul* 8.77, 61.

5. Joseph of Panephysis 7, in *The Sayings of the Desert Fathers*, trans. Benedicta Ward (Cistercian Publications, 1975), 103.

6. A. W. Tozer, *God's Pursuit of Man* (Moody, 2015), 105.

VULNERABLE

1. Jacques Ellul, *The Subversion of Christianity*, trans. Geoffrey W. Bromiley (Eerdmans, 1986), 124.

2. Dorothy Day, "Quote/Unquote," In Communion, accessed March 12, 2026, https://incommunion.org/2004/12/05/quote-unquote-2.

3. Tertullian, *On Idolatry*, in *Ante-Nicene Fathers*, vol. 3, trans. S. Thelwall (Christian Literature, 1885), 73.

4. Athanasius, *On the Incarnation*, trans. John Behr (St. Vladimir's Seminary Press, 2011), 109.

5. Todd M. Johnson, "Christian Martyrdom: Who? Why? How?" Gordon-Conwell Theological Seminary, December 18, 2019, https://www.gordonconwell.edu/blog/christian-martyrdom-who-why-how.

ONE

1. George MacDonald, *George MacDonald: An Anthology*, ed. C. S. Lewis (HarperCollins, 2001), 77.

KENNETH TANNER is pastor of Church of the Holy Redeemer in Rochester Hills, Michigan, where he has served since 2005. His writing has appeared in many outlets, including *Huffington Post*, *Sojourners*, *Mockingbird*, *National Review*, *Christianity Today*, *Clarion Journal*, and more. He and his wife, Debbie, have seven children and four grandchildren.

CONNECT WITH KENNETH

@kennethtanner

kenneth.tanner

@kentanner

@kentanner

@kennethtanner